Spanish-American War

Spanish-American War

UPDATED EDITION

MICHAEL GOLAY

JOHN S. BOWMAN
GENERAL EDITOR

Facts On File, Inc.

Note on Photos
Many of the illustrations and photographs used in this book are old,
historical images. The quality of the prints is not always up to modern
standards, as in some cases the originals are from glass negatives or are damaged.
The content of the illustrations, however, made their inclusion important
despite problems in reproduction.

Facts On File, Inc.
132 West 31st Street
New York NY 10001

Library of Congress Cataloging-in-Publication Data

Golay, Michael, 1951–
Spanish-American War / by Michael Golay. — Updated ed.
p. cm. — (America at war)
Summary: A narrative account of the Spanish American War,
covering the origins of dispute between the United States and Spain over Cuba,
profiles of the key figures, and descriptions of major battles.
Includes bibliographical references and index.
ISBN 0-8160-4935-1
1. Spanish-American War, 1898—Juvenile literature. [1. Spanish-American War,
1898.] I. Title. II. Series.
E715.G58 2003
973.8'9—dc21   2002008764

Facts On File books are available at special discounts when purchased in bulk
quantities for businesses, associations, institutions, or sales promotions. Please call our
Special Sales Department in New York at (212) 967-8800 or (800) 322-8755.

You can find Facts On File on the World Wide Web at http://www.factsonfile.com

Text design by Erika K. Arroyo
Logo design by Smart Graphics
Maps by Jeremy Eagle

Printed in the United States of America

MP FOF 10 9 8 7 6 5 4 3 2 1

This book is printed on acid-free paper.

Contents

Preface

Historians find it convenient to present 1898, the year of the war between the United States and Spain over Cuba, as a great divide in the American narrative—"that special conjuncture," in the words of Louis Pérez, Jr., "that often serves to delineate one historical epoch from another." They identify the year and its short, sharp, decisive war as marking the moment when the United States emerged as a world power. The events of 1898, the consensus says, changed the course of American history and foreshadowed the ascent of the United States to superpower status.

David Traxel expresses this commonly held notion in *1898: The Birth of the American Century,* one of a number of works to appear in the centennial year of the Spanish-American War:

> During twelve months of rich confusion, wild contradiction, and violent change, the United States in 1898 advanced from being viewed as a country of sharp-dealing businessmen with a second-rate military and little international influence to acknowledgment as a respected member of the imperialists' club, alongside Great Britain, France, Japan, and Germany. It was the first and necessary step in making the twentieth century the American century.

In this view, one fateful year changed everything.

Centennials are often the occasion for reconsideration of historical events, and they also tend to put new perspectives on books such as the first edition of this one—highlighting old themes, asking new questions. The events of 1898 were the product of historical forces that had been building for a generation. Nor did Americans all of a sudden begin to look outward on January 1, 1898. The Monroe Doctrine—the claim of U.S. primacy in the Americas and the diplomatic justification for longtime U.S. interest in the island of Cuba—dated from 1821. And it was American adventurers who stirred up trouble on the island in the 1850s. Writing in 1859, William Seward, who would become Abraham Lincoln's secretary of state, regarded eventual U.S. annexation of Cuba as a given: "Every rock and every grain of sand in that island were drifted and washed out of American soil by the floods of the Mississippi, and other estuaries of the Gulf of Mexico. The island has seemed to me, just as our predecessors have said, to gravitate back again to the parent continent from which it sprang." Seward is remembered mostly for his acquisition of Alaska for the United States in 1867. But his vision penetrated far beyond the continent, across the Pacific to Japan and China, whose markets eventually would be deemed essential to U.S. prosperity.

Economic interests, prestige, and domestic politics combined in the latter decades of the 19th century to propel the Americans beyond their shores. Cuba indirectly spurred the 1880s expansion of U.S. naval power. In 1873, during the Ten Years' War, the first war for Cuban independence, the Spanish seized the gun-running U.S. ship *Virginius,* declared the vessel a pirate, and executed its captain along with 53 crew members and suspected guerrillas. A British warship calling at the Cuban port of Santiago protested sharply and saved another 155 passengers from execution. In response, the United States could only manage to assemble a few obsolescent American warships at Key West, Florida.

"We remained several weeks, making faces at the Spaniards 90 miles away in Havana, while two modern vessels would have done us up in 30 minutes," wrote Lt. Robley Evans, who would command a powerful U.S. battleship off Cuba in the 1898 war. "We were dreadfully mortified over it all."

Memories of the *Virginius* affair were still fresh a decade later when an alliance of business interests, naval officers, and expansionist politicians pressed for a U.S. naval buildup. (See "The New Navy," Chapter 1) Perceived affronts to national dignity abroad generated popular support for the construction of a modern fleet. In Samoa during the winter of 1888–89, an American, German, and British dispute over the use of the islands as a naval station threatened to break out into open conflict. A powerful ocean storm knocked out the Americans before any shots were exchanged, sinking two of the three obsolete wooden vessels of the U.S. squadron. And in the Chilean port of Valparaiso in 1890, mobs with the passive consent of local police attacked U.S. sailors on shore leave from the cruiser *Baltimore,* killing two and injuring 36. This incident, too, seemed to underline the need for powerful naval forces to protect U.S. interests and prestige.

The United States in the 1890s was a growing nation, an increasingly urban and industrial society. Despite a severe economic depression beginning in 1893, U.S. national wealth approached the astonishing figure of $65 billion—higher than Britain's, higher than Germany's and Russia's *combined.* All this wealth, though, was unevenly distributed: The richest 1 percent of Americans claimed the same total income as the bottom 50 percent of the population. A skilled worker in the 1890s earned about three dollars a day for a 10-hour day; unskilled workers took home half that much. The U.S. population approached 75 million, with immigration—much of it from southern and eastern Europe—accounting for most of the increase from the previous decade. Imbalance of wealth, mass immigration, the recurrent cycles of economic boom and bust, and the social strains these forces created made the America of the 1890s an anxious land.

In widely discussed writings early in the 1890s, a historian and a naval officer sought to make sense of the past, assess the present, and show the way forward into a prosperous and powerful American future. Taken together, the historian, Frederick Jackson Turner, and the naval officer, Alfred Thayer Mahan, provided the philosophical foundation for aggressive American overseas expansion.

In a lecture delivered at the World's Columbian Exposition in Chicago in 1893, Turner argued that the frontier conditioned the American character and the course of American democracy. "Up to our own day American history has been in a large degree the history of the colonization of the Great West," Turner wrote. "The existence of an area of free land, its continuous recession, and the advance of American settlement westward, explain American development." The empty lands filled up in the decades after the Civil War and the Census of 1890 formally declared the frontier closed. Turner predicted that America would explore new avenues of development rather than suffer eventual economic and political decline. "He would be a rash prophet who should assert that the expansive character of American life has now entirely ceased," he wrote. "Movement has been its dominant fact, and, unless this training has no effect upon a people, the American energy will continually demand a wider field for its exercise." Expansionists read into Turner a necessity to push beyond the continental landmass—specifically, across the Pacific.

Mahan, a career naval officer, long had brooded on the role of maritime power in the development of nations. In the introduction to his book *The Influence of Sea Power upon History* (1890), he argued that geography, a maritime tradition, national character, and democratic political institutions uniquely positioned the United States for world leadership. He suggested, too, that the powerful American economy would soon produce more than Americans could absorb. Thus overseas markets were necessary for economic growth, strong naval forces were necessary to open foreign markets and protect them, and overseas outposts—colonies, in fact—were necessary to sustain the fleets. "Whether they will or no, Americans must now begin to look outward," wrote Mahan.

Turner and Mahan deeply influenced political leaders of the late 1890s, among them President William McKinley; Henry Cabot Lodge, a Massachusetts senator and a leading spokesman for the expansionists in Congress; and Theodore Roosevelt, a rising political star whose name, bumptious personality, and bespectacled visage would become inextricably linked with the events of 1898. McKinley, although unassertive by nature, allowed the expansionists to maneuver him into the annexation of Hawaii in 1898. Lodge argued forcefully from 1895 on for U.S. support of Cuban independence. Roosevelt, a blunt, energetic, and compulsive adventurer, saw armed conflict as necessary and desirable in the life of nations.

"I should welcome almost any war for I think this country needs one," he said in 1897 when, as assistant secretary of the navy, he found himself in a position to influence U.S. strategic policy.

Roosevelt, his "Rough Riders" volunteer cavalry regiment, and Roosevelt crony John Hay's description of the conflict as that "splendid little war" long defined the Spanish-American confrontation in popular image. Even in scholarly treatments, the figure of Roosevelt towers over events, partly, perhaps, because he was one of the first to write about them, in his book *The Rough Riders,* rushed into print before the critical year came to an end. The large contingent of journalists who followed U.S. forces also helped shape the view of the war as an adventure, although Richard Harding Davis and others, true to their muckraking heritage, attacked incompetence and corruption in the high command even as they glamorized Roosevelt.

A revision of this rather frivolous view of events came in 1931 with Walter Millis's skeptical, cool *The Martial Spirit.* For all his ironic tone,

Millis (or his publisher) still chose to present a photograph of Roosevelt in his Rough Rider costume as the frontispiece of the book. All the same, the looming tragedy of World War I infuses *The Martial Spirit*. Millis presented the shapers of events in 1898 as representative of the country at large: unreflective, innocent, anxious, aware of great changes in the land but uncertain of where they would lead. Americans seemed, too, to have blanked out visions of war's real face, as their fathers and brothers had seen it during the Civil War, at Spotsylvania, Cold Harbor, and Petersburg in Virginia.

"A new, post-war generation had grown up into the seats of power or their ante-rooms," Millis wrote. "Its history had been written and read; its passions were fading, and its pain, especially, had been forgotten. . . . As a nation we were not sure of ourselves, of where we stood, or of what was happening to us."

Millis emphasized confusion, incompetence, and corruption on both sides of the conflict. Writing a generation and a second world war later, Frank Friedel in 1958 sought to redress what he regarded as an imbalance in the historical accounts, titling his book, without any apparent ironic intent, *The Splendid Little War*. While far from ignoring the disreputable aspects of the conflict, he tended to accept the main actors at their own valuation.

"The slogans, aspirations and chivalry of the combatants seemed as quaintly antique as gaslight," Friedel wrote of the post–World War I view. "In jeering at what had been spurious or ridiculous, Americans unfortunately overlooked the idealism, fortitude and even heroism of tens of thousands of their fellows who sought to free Cuba and destroy Spanish power in Puerto Rico and the Philippines in 1898."

In *The Tragedy of American Diplomacy*, published a year after Friedel's book, William Appleman Williams explored ulterior or hidden motivations of Americans of 1898. "It is clear that various groups saw war with Spain over Cuba as a means to solve other problems," Williams wrote. "Agrarians viewed it as a way to monetize silver at home and thus pave the way for a general expansion of their exports. Some labor groups thought it would ease or resolve immediate economic difficulties. And many important businessmen came to support war for specific commercial purposes as well as general economic reasons." In Williams's view, the venture seemed less an accident, an inevitability, or a spontaneous crusade to free the Cubans than a calculated response to specific, mostly economic, issues.

There were strategic issues as well, for Cuba in the hands of a hostile power could threaten the canal connecting the Atlantic and the Pacific that the U.S. hoped to build in Central America. (See "The Voyage of the *Oregon,*" Chapter 7) Nevertheless, with all their differences of emphasis and style, most historians agree that the United States went to war to free the island from a colonial oppressor. David Trask, in *The War with Spain in 1898* (1981), styled the conflict as a humanitarian crusade with the aim of liberating Cuba. "The Spanish American War was fought to free Cuba," John Garraty wrote in *A Short History of the American Nation* (1993).

Whatever their different interpretations of U.S. involvement in the Spanish-American War, historians agree that it was a watershed event. "For the United States it was metamorphosis, the shell of isolation was broken and a new American dominion suddenly stretched from the Caribbean to the Far East," G. J. A. O'Toole wrote in *The Spanish War* in 1984. "It was a national rite of passage, transforming a former colony into a world power." Beyond this consensus, some historians began paying closer attention to Cuban and Spanish sources and points of view, placing the American emergence in a broader context. Moreover, recent scholarship fully acknowledges the Cuban insurgent contribution to the war. The Cubans inflicted thousands of casualties on the Spanish and—perhaps more significant—obliged them to disperse their forces in small fixed garrisons defending population centers. "By July 1898, the Spanish army in Cuba [had been reduced] to a state of offensive impotence," historian John Scott Reed wrote in 1994. Insurgent military operations left the Spanish too scattered and too demoralized to mount an effective challenge to the U.S. landing on the island's south coast.

As Louis Pérez notes in *The War of 1898* (1998), the episode marked a great divide for Spain as well: The U.S. conquest ended five centuries of Spanish empire in the New World. And for Cuba (independence and eventual revolution), Puerto Rico (the modified colonial relationship with the United States that exists today) and the Philippines (U.S. colonial rule, rebellion, eventual independence), 1898 proved fateful, too. It is only proper that readers of this book be reminded that what at first might seem like a minor and remote war set up reverberations that continue to make headlines to this day.

U.S. relations with the three countries were often difficult throughout the 20th century and remain unsettled into the 21st century. In Cuba, American-sponsored insurgencies sought in the early 1960s to

PREFACE

topple the communist government of Fidel Castro, and the U.S. government continues, directly as well as indirectly, to support those Cubans who challenge Castro's rule. The United States and the Soviet Union nearly went to war in 1962 over the placement of Soviet nuclear weapons on the island. The United States continues its economic embargo against Cuba in the new century, while many thousands of Cuban immigrants in the United States wield a disproportionate influence on U.S. politics because of "the Cuban question."

Puerto Rico also remains an unresolved legacy from the Spanish-American War. In a series of island-wide referendums, Puerto Ricans have turned down U.S. statehood while supporting their country's commonwealth status, but this has not prevented *independistas* from resorting to violence to promote their crusade for a totally independent Puerto Rico. Protesters continue to confront the U.S. military in its use of the Puerto Rican island of Vieques as a firing range.

The Philippines would seem to be the one major acquisition of the Spanish-American War with which the United States has enjoyed uncomplicated relations. Up to a point this has been true, for it was a relationship tested and strengthened by World War II. But some Filipinos have not forgotten that the United States at least indirectly supported the dictatorship of Ferdinand Marcos (1965–86). Undoubtedly this influenced the Filipino demand that the United States close down all its military bases in the islands during the 1990s. In the aftermath of the attack on the World Trade Center in 2001, U.S. forces did return to the Philippines, a potential battlefield in President George W. Bush's war on terrorism. Officials of both governments insisted that U.S. troops were there solely in an advisory capacity in the fight against another Philippine insurrection, this one Muslim-inspired, but many Filipinos remain uneasy with the reappearance of U.S. military in their land.

Current events rekindled interest in this brief war of more than a century ago. Two new general histories of the Spanish-American War appeared in 1998, the centennial year, Traxel's *1898: The Birth of the American Century* and Ivan Musicant's *Empire by Default: The Spanish-American War and the Dawn of the American Century.* Perhaps because, at bottom, the 1898 war seems a straightforward (if not splendid) affair, book titles also tend to be simple and uncomplicated. Traxel's reflects the broad notion of America's rather sudden emergence as a force in the world. Musicant's casts the United States in a passive role, suggesting—in a position opposed to that of William Appleman Williams—that the

Americans rose to world leadership and acquired a colonial empire largely by historical accident.

Perhaps because of its brevity, the Spanish-American War has attracted scant interest from filmmakers, even though it became the first American war in which motion picture cameras were used. A Library of Congress website, "The Spanish-American War in Motion Pictures," offers online access to these grainy, jerky, and fascinating newsreels. A Turner Films miniseries, *The Rough Riders* (2001) is available on video, as is a fine centennial Public Broadcasting Service documentary, *The Crucible of Empire: The Spanish-American War.*

A sampling of the many websites now available might include, along with the aforementioned Library of Congress website, the following: "The World of 1898: The Spanish-American War," with an overview essay, chronology, documents in Spanish and English, and a bibliography (Library of Congress); "A War in Perspective, 1898–1998: Public Appeals, Memory and the Spanish-American Conflict" (New York Public Library); and "The Most Dreadful Pest of Humanity: Yellow Fever and the Reed Commission, 1898–1901" (University of Virginia).

This updated edition of *Spanish-American War* contains substantial new material—this preface, short essays within each chapter highlighting aspects of the basic narrative, new maps, new illustrations, and an expanded reading list. As one reads, connections with the recent past may become evident. The destruction of a highly visible symbol of American power, the battleship *Maine,* and the attendant loss of life stirred the nation to an immediate and overwhelming military response. The memory of the appalling casualties of the Civil War led U.S. commanders in Cuba to pursue indirect means of defeating the enemy—by siege rather than frontal assault. The analogies are far from exact—Havana and lower Manhattan, a warship and a skyscraper, Vietnam and Afghanistan, a siege and a cruise missile—are quite different things. But Americans are the sum of their past, and so it is natural to view the present and the future through the lens of history.

Prologue

Death of a Battleship

The USS *Maine* steamed back and forth off Havana, Cuba, marking time. The battleship's commander, Capt. Charles Sigsbee, waited until the sun had climbed well above the horizon before instructing the helmsman to steer for the harbor. "I did not desire to reach Havana at early daylight," Sigsbee explained later, "but rather to steam in when the town was alive and on its feet." Havanans watching from the crowded waterfront's cafes, offices, and warehouses could hardly fail to be impressed. The 319-foot-long warship, in its elegant peacetime paint scheme of bright white hull, straw-colored superstructure, and black masts, stacks, and guns, glided through the narrow harbor entrance and moored at Buoy 4. After an exchange of salutes with the Spanish man-of-war *Alfonso XII*, Sigsbee passed the word for the *Maine*'s awnings to be rigged to shade the crew from the ferocious sun.

Havana was peaceful that morning, January 25, 1898, though the Cuban rebellion continued to claim its daily tribute of victims. Cubans had been fighting to free themselves of Spanish colonial rule since early 1895. The United States showed keen interest in the affairs of the island, located just 90 miles south of Key West, Florida. Americans sympathized with Cuban political aspirations. They found Spanish methods of putting down the insurgency repugnant, especially the forced resettlement of country people in fortified towns—*reconcentrado,* in Spanish. Beyond that, Americans had substantial economic investments on the island. Momentum seemed to be building for some form of United States intervention in the conflict.

The *Maine* came to Havana not only to protect American lives and property, but also as a symbol of U.S. power. Fitzhugh Lee, the chief U.S.

The *Maine* enters the harbor of Havana in January 1898.
(National Archives/DOD, War & Conflict #0207)

diplomatic representative in Cuba, had been campaigning for just such a presence for months. Lee, who had commanded cavalry in the Confederate army of his uncle, Gen. Robert E. Lee, during the U.S. Civil War, believed the Spanish were incapable of pacifying the island. Ultimately,

PROLOGUE

he thought, the United States would have to impose a settlement, by force if necessary.

As a preliminary step, the U.S. Navy in October 1897 detached the *Maine* from the North Atlantic Squadron, instructed Sigsbee to keep the ship's bunkers topped off with coal, and alerted him for a possible southward move. In mid-December Sigsbee took the *Maine* to Key West, only six hours steaming time from Havana. In mid-January, mobs of *peninsulares*—natives of Spain permanently settled on the island— rioted in the Cuban capital in protest against the Spanish home government's steps toward a form of political autonomy for the colony. Though no Americans were injured (or even threatened) in the disturbances, President William McKinley decided to act.

Suddenly turning cautious, Lee advised that sending a ship in the aftermath of the riots might increase the likelihood of trouble. He recommended waiting another week or so. McKinley ordered the *Maine* to Havana anyway—for, as he put it, "a friendly interchange of calls with the authorities." He meant this to be a measured response to the crisis. The *Maine* was an impressive vessel, but McKinley could have sent a larger, faster, more powerful one. Built to an already out-of-date pattern and commissioned in 1895, the *Maine* was rated a second-class battleship. Still, at 6,700 tons, carrying four 10-inch guns in two turrets and capable of steaming at 17 knots, it could overwhelm any ship in the Spanish fleet.

Cuba's Spanish rulers let U.S. diplomats know that they would view a visit from the *Maine* as an unfriendly act. Hence, official Spanish greetings as the warship dropped anchor on January 25 were chilly, though strictly proper. The mobs did not gather. "Ship arrived quietly 11 A.M. today," Lee cabled the State Department. "No demonstrations so far." But Sigsbee took every precaution. He confined the 354-man crew to the ship. He posted armed sentries and saw to it that ammunition for the six-pounder deck guns lay at hand. The engineers were told to keep up sufficient steam to power the gun turrets. Even the peddlers in small boats were chased away.

Sigsbee, a 53-year-old Civil War veteran and a noted deep-sea explorer, had taken command of the *Maine* in 1897. He doubtless knew something of its unlucky history. Fire had broken out aboard while it was under construction in the New York Navy Yard. In February 1896 it ran aground. A year later five bluejackets, as U.S. sailors were called, were swept from its decks during a storm off Cape Hatteras. But the chances of accident seemed remote here in this palmy anchorage. Things remained calm ashore, too, and in early February Washington considered withdrawing the *Maine*. Consul Lee objected. "We are masters of the situation now and I would not disturb or alter it," he advised.

Relations with the Spanish authorities grew cordial. Sigsbee exchanged visits with the ranking Spanish admiral. Spanish government and army officers visited the ship. Sigsbee and several of his officers went ashore to attend a bullfight. A Spanish general sent a case of fine sherry to Sigsbee, who returned the favor with a copy of his book, *Deep Sea Sounding and Dredging*. There were Americans to entertain, too: Fitz Lee, of course, and Clara Barton of the American Red Cross, who was in Havana to distribute food and medicines to Cuban war victims. Sigsbee gave her lunch on board.

February 15, 1898, passed much like the preceding days. The tropical sun set in a brief, spectacular blaze. The evening was calm, hot, sultry. In his cabin, Sigsbee put aside a memorandum on torpedoes and began a letter to his wife. As he wrote, the ship's bugler played Taps; it was, the captain wrote, "singularly beautiful in the oppressive stillness of the night." Then, as he sealed the letter, he heard a dull roar and felt a sudden shock. The lights went out. There were screams, shouts of confusion, the rush of water somewhere below.

"The city shook to a terrific explosion," wrote *New York Herald* correspondent Walter Scott Meriwether, who had just taken a seat in a Havana café. "Amid a shower of falling plaster every light in the place went out, as did every other electric light in the city." Meriwether ran into the street and followed the crowds toward the bright yellow glow beyond the waterfront.

Red Cross headquarters rocked with what Clara Barton, at work there, believed at first to be a stupendous clap of thunder. She looked out the windows. "Out over the bay," she wrote, "the air was filled with a blaze of light, and this in turn was filled with black specks like huge specters flying in all directions. Then it faded away, the bells rang, the whistles blew, and voices in the street were heard for a moment; then all was quiet again."

Aboard the Ward Line steamer *City of Washington,* moored a few hundred yards from the *Maine,* passenger Sigmund Rothschild felt an explosion, looked up, and saw the bow of the warship rise ghostly out of the water. A second detonation followed, then a sheet of flame amidships. "Everything went over our heads, a black mass," he wrote. "We could not tell what it was. It was all black. Then we heard the noise of falling material."

Sigsbee rushed out onto the main deck, already awash, and confusedly called out orders to repel boarders. There was, in fact, little left to board, and anyway the enemy turned out to be a phantom. The ship was sinking rapidly under him. He could make out dark forms in the water. Two undamaged ship's boats were lowered; rescue craft shortly arrived from the *City of Washington* and the *Alfonso XII.* Fire reached the six-pounder ammunition, which was stored on deck, and it began to explode, shell by shell.

The blast had occurred in the forward part of the ship, where nearly all of the *Maine*'s 328 sailors were berthed. The *Herald*'s Meriwether, meantime, had rowed out to the *City of Washington,* where some of the wounded had been taken. "Most of the victims were either dead or dying and only one was able to talk coherently," Meriwether reported. "All he knew was that he was asleep in his hammock when he was hurled high in the air by a terrific explosion, had struck the water, and someone had rescued him." Spanish doctors summoned from shore worked furiously to save as many of the wounded as possible. Meriwether watched a surgeon dress the destroyed face of one of the *Maine*'s firemen. "'There is something in my eyes,' he said. 'Wait and let me open them.' Both eyes were gone."

The *Maine* settled into the harbor mud. Sigsbee stepped off the poop deck, now only a few inches above the waterline, and into one of the

The USS *Maine* blows up, February 15, 1898. *(Library of Congress)*

small boats. It carried him to the *City of Washington*, where he prepared the following cable:

> *Maine* blown up in Havana harbor at nine forty to-night and destroyed. Many wounded and doubtless more killed or drowned. Wounded and others aboard Spanish man-of-war and Ward Line steamer. Send Light House Tenders from Key West for crew and the few pieces of equipment above water. No one has clothing other than that upon him. Public opinion should be suspended until further report. All officers believed saved. Many Spanish officers . . . now with us to express sympathy.

In fact, two of the *Maine*'s 28 officers were dead; 264 enlisted men had been killed or mortally injured. And Sigsbee could hardly suspend his own judgment as to the cause. "I surmised from the first," he wrote afterward, "that the explosion initiated from outside the vessel." Captain Sigsbee thought someone—he was not prepared to assign blame—had blown up his ship with a submarine mine.

PROLOGUE

A journalist took Sigsbee's cable ashore. Dispatched from Havana around 11:00 P.M., it reached Navy Secretary John Long in Washington at 1:30 A.M. Long ordered the lighthouse tenders to sail for Havana and telephoned word of the disaster to President McKinley. Awakened by the report, the president could only pace the floor and mutter (an aide later reported), "The *Maine* blown up! The *Maine* blown up!" The news made the late editions of the morning papers, pushing nearly everything else off the front page.

The Purloined Letter

IN THE COMPETITION FOR READERS IN THE LATE 19TH century, the editors of sensationalist newspapers would stop at nothing short of breaking and entering—and perhaps not even there—to gain attention. As the crisis with Spain over Cuba developed, some stories bore only a passing connection with reality.

Joseph Pulitzer and William Randolph Hearst, publishers of rival newspapers, the *World* and the *New York Journal* respectively, were locked in a fierce circulation battle in 1898. Hearst would even claim credit for the war with Spain. In May, a few weeks after the outbreak of the fighting, he asked his readers in bold type on page 1: "How do you like the *Journal's* war?"

Three months earlier, Hearst's paper had scored one of the scoops of the crisis and at the same time sharply increased tensions between the United States and Spain. On February 9, 1898, the *Journal* published an only too genuine private letter from Enrique Dupuy de Lôme, Spain's ambassador to the United States, to José Canalejas, a Spanish journalist and politician in Madrid. In the letter, Dupuy de Lôme dismissed President William McKinley as "weak and catering to the rabble, and besides, a low politician who desires to . . . stand well with the jingoes of his party."

An employee of Canalejas who sympathized with the Cuban rebels had stolen the letter and immediately sailed for New York; there he gave it to other rebel supporters, who brought it to Hearst. He splashed the story on page 1 for five days. Dupuy de Lôme, anticipating a tremendous stir, resigned at once; the scandal proved short-lived, however. The explosion of the battleship *Maine* less than a week later drove Dupuy de Lôme's indiscretion off the front pages and propelled the United States and Spain into war.

Official U.S. reaction was cautious. At first, expert naval opinion leaned toward the theory that spontaneous combustion of bunker coal had touched off an explosion in one of the ship's powder magazines. There had been reports of bunker fires on several U.S. warships in recent years, though all had been discovered and extinguished before any damage could be done. This seemed the most likely cause of the *Maine*'s death.

But America's influential "yellow press"—the scandal and sensation sheets, especially the rival New York newspapers of Joseph Pulitzer and William Randolph Hearst—came to an independent conclusion. Treachery had sunk the *Maine*. "THE WAR SHIP MAINE WAS SPLIT IN TWO BY AN ENEMY'S SECRET INFERNAL MACHINE," Hearst's *New York Journal* declared boldly, in big black headlines that could admit of no doubt. The crisis over Cuba, building gradually and steadily for many years, now seemed about to explode into war.

1

CROSSFIRE

Spain, Cuba, the United States

By the mid-1890s, a generation of Cubans had known an uneasy calm. A decade-long rebellion against Spanish authority in Cuba ended in 1878 when the exhausted adversaries negotiated a fragile compromise peace. Although the Ten Years' War did lead to the emancipation of Cuba's slaves, Spain failed to keep most of its promises of political reform for the island. The Treaty of Zanjón which ended the revolt would prove to be merely a 17-year cease-fire.

Spain's long imperial relationship with Cuba stretched back to 1492, the year Christopher Columbus landed on the island during his first voyage of discovery to what Europeans called the New World. He found a fertile land 750 miles long and, on average, 50 miles wide, with wild mountains, dense tropical forests, and rolling prairies. Soldiers and colonists soon followed. The first permanent Spanish settlements were established in 1511. The Spanish dominated the native Taino Indians and, within a few years, were importing the first slaves from Africa. Spanish overlords eventually made Cuba the richest and most populous of all the West Indian islands. The Spanish came to call it the "Pearl of the Antilles."

As the 19th century neared its end, Cuba's population approached 1.5 million. The Taino had long since been killed off or absorbed into the general population, which at the time of the *Maine* incident included 200,000 Spaniards, 500,000 descendants of African slaves, and 800,000 Cuban-born whites. Those of direct Spanish descent, the *peninsulares*, held nearly all of the island's economic power; political power remained seated in Spain. Some Cubans, white and black, had mounted challenges

José Martí (1853–1895)
(Library of Congress)

to the political arrangements over the years, even before the Ten Years' War. Now Cuban rebels were stirring again.

The immediate causes were economic. Prices for the island's chief product, sugar, had fallen to the lowest levels on record, largely in reaction to a steep new U.S. import duty. The Spanish retaliated by increasing tariffs on American goods sold in Cuba. The trade war caused a painful rise in the Cuban cost of living. Meanwhile, the Spanish political administration remained corrupt and inefficient. Determined to exploit political grievances as well as economic hardships, a rebel alliance in February 1895 issued a proclamation known as the Grito de Baire (or "outcry of Baire," after the town in which the insurgents issued it). The leader of this call for a second war for independence was a former political prisoner, José Martí.

The Cuban-born son of a Spanish soldier, Martí was 17 years old in 1870 when the colonial authorities arrested him on a Havana street for taunting a column of Spanish troops sent to the island during the Ten

Years' War. By war's end, Martí had spent a year in jail without trial and another six years at hard labor in Spain. Barred from Cuba, he moved restlessly from place to place: Madrid, the Spanish capital, where he briefly studied literature and law, then Mexico, Guatemala, and Venezuela. Then, in 1881, he moved to the United States.

Martí found his vocation in America, among the 20,000 Cuban emigrés of Tampa, Key West, New Orleans, Chicago, and New York City. Preaching unity and cooperation among Cuba's divided social and racial classes, he worked tirelessly to mobilize emigré resources for a renewal of the rebellion.

His Cuban Revolutionary Party, formally established in 1892, sought money for arms from Cuban Americans and courted powerful allies in American labor organizations and the press. Though he welcomed American material and moral support, Martí urged Cubans to win the struggle by themselves, without direct American intervention. Influential lobbies in America favored U.S. annexation of the island. "Once the United States is in Cuba," Martí asked, "who will get her out?" For now, he wanted nothing more from America than cash to buy the weapons of war.

In early April 1895, Martí and the insurrection's senior military commander, Máximo Gómez, came ashore on Cuba's lightly settled southeast coast. Though no soldier, Martí had determined on a share of the fighting. "I called up the war," he explained. "My responsibility begins rather than ends with it." Gómez launched a series of guerrilla raids in Oriente Province in the eastern part of the island. Within a few weeks of the outbreak, Spanish cavalry patrols claimed their most celebrated victim. On May 19, firing from ambush, they shot and killed José Martí near the village of Dos Ríos. He was 42 years old.

Gómez, who had been a senior rebel commander in the Ten Years' War, succeeded Martí as the central figure of the rebellion. The son of a Spanish army officer, he was a gray little man, unimpressive in his ill-fitting clothes. But Gómez had great prestige among the *insurrectos*. His strategy aimed to make the island useless to Spain by ransacking its economy. "The chains of Cuba have been forged by her own richness," he said. Gómez paid particular attention to sugar, which accounted for 75 percent of Cuba's wealth and was the main source of Spanish revenue. He ordered the burning of cane fields and sugar mills. Field and factory workers who failed to cooperate in the destruction of their own livelihoods were to be shot.

This lithograph attests to the popularity of "Cuba's heroes" in 1896: Máximo Gómez, Gen. Antonio Maceo, José Martí, Salvador Cisneros, and Gen. Calixto García. *(Library of Congress, Prints & Photographs Division [LC-USZ62-101602])*

A Spanish officer left this description of the methods used by members of Gómez's Liberating Army:

> They frequently rest during the day, and march at night, in as light order as possible, carrying only a hammock, a piece of oilcloth, cartridges, machete, and rifle. They live by marauding. The country people feed them, and help them so far as they can, and where these insurgents don't find sympathy, the machete, the torch, and the rope are good arguments.

The Cubans used hit-and-run tactics, avoiding direct, open-field encounters with Spanish regular troops. The rebels were short of arms, ammunition, clothing, food, and medicine. They had no artillery. One insurgent column obtained a rusted cannon, said to date from Columbus's time. The rebels trundled it along as a sort of mascot. One man cleaned it, scavenged powder and balls, and test-fired it. The piece blew up on the second firing.

Often the rebels were armed only with the machete, "a formidable chopper-sword," in the words of Winston S. Churchill, who as a young British army officer accompanied a Spanish mobile column as an observer in the autumn of 1895. On leave from the army and in Cuba strictly on his own, Churchill found himself in sympathy with the Spanish, likening their difficulties in Cuba to his own country's troubles with the unappeasable Irish.

"They moved league after league, day after day, through a world of impalpable hostility, slashed here and there by fierce onslaught," Britain's future World War II leader wrote of the Spanish forces. Churchill saw his first combat in a short, sharp exchange with rebels in a jungle clearing near the mid-island town of Sancti Spiritus. "It really seemed dangerous indeed, and I was astonished to see how few people were hit in all this clatter," he wrote afterward. Churchill sensed the Spaniards' frustrations. They could not get a firm hold on their elusive enemy. After a few volleys, the Cubans stopped firing and disappeared into the jungle. The Spaniards made no attempt to follow.

The Spanish captain general of Cuba, Arsenio Martínez Campos, soon admitted that the military problem was beyond his capabilities. Campos had led Spanish forces to victory in the Ten Years' War, but the war of the 1890s was a more bitter, more violent and far deadlier conflict. Spanish troops held the cities and garrison towns. The insurgents ruled the countryside. Campos's system of *trochas,* fortified defensive belts 200 yards wide that, in one place, stretched across Cuba's full 50-mile width, sought to confine the rebels to the east end of the island. In fact, Gómez's cavalry penetrated the *trochas* almost at will.

Reinforcements from Spain were not the solution. The conscripts were more susceptible than the native Cubans to fevers and other tropical diseases. Someone asked Gómez to name his best generals: "June, July and August," he answered—the yellow fever months.

In December 1895, Gómez's brilliant second-in-command, Antonio Maceo, a descendant of African slaves, launched an invasion of the western provinces. With 1,500 cavalrymen, Maceo cut a wide swath of destruction through the countryside, burning fields, farms, and mills, tearing up railroad track, and taking down telegraph lines. On January 22, 1896, his mounted columns reached Mantua, the westernmost town in Cuba.

By then Campos, conceding defeat, had resigned his command. To replace him, Madrid sent a hard-handed officer of Prussian background, Gen. Valeriano Weyler y Nicolau. Before leaving, Campos had suggested trying a harsh new policy, *reconcentración,* in which the country people were to be relocated within the Spanish lines. Such a policy would deny food, shelter, and other aid to the insurgents, and discourage new recruits. In proposing the policy, Campos admitted that he lacked the ruthlessness to carry it out. And he had little faith that *reconcentración* would work in any event. "Even if the insurgents are beaten in the field or forced into submission, my loyal and sincere opinion is that we will have another war within ten years; and if we still did no more than shed our blood, there would be another and another and another," Campos wrote the Madrid authorities. "Can Spain afford to go on like this?"

Weyler thought Spain could; besides, he had few of Campos's scruples. He landed at Havana on February 10, 1896, and immediately issued a series of *reconcentración* orders. Weyler also strengthened the *trocha* system, reinforcing the garrisons and fitting out the defenses with electric searchlights.

Some 500,000 Cubans eventually ended up in the concentration camps. Many internees were without shelters. Food was scarce. Medical and sanitary services were primitive. Casualty figures could only be guessed, but estimates of the number of deaths resulting from the *reconcentración* policy ranged into the hundreds of thousands. The American observer William J. Calhoun described the effects:

> The country outside of the military posts was practically depopulated. Every house had been burned, banana trees cut down, cane fields swept with fire, and everything in the shape of food destroyed. I did not see a house, man, woman or child, horse, mule or cow, nor even a dog. I did not see a sign of life, except an occasional vulture or buzzard sailing through the air. The country was wrapped in the stillness of death and the silence of desolation.

On the insurgent side, the scorched earth policies of Gómez were equally harsh and equally effective. Cuba's agricultural economy was ravaged. The value of the island's sugar crop plummeted to $13 million in 1896, down from as much as $60 million in peak years. "Poverty and misery are everywhere apparent," the London *Times* reported in June 1896, 15 months after the outbreak of the rebellion. "Families who were in comfortable and even wealthy circumstances a year ago now wonder where they can obtain the wherewithal to buy the necessities of life."

Weyler scored some limited successes. Maceo, the "Bronze Titan," was killed in an ambush near Havana in early December 1896, a grievous loss for Gómez. Yet despite the presence of 160,000 Spanish troops, the insurgents continued to control most of the eastern half of the island. Maceo's cavalry columns, though now deprived of their leader, still operated in the western provinces.

To the north, beyond the Florida Strait, Americans closely followed the progress of the rebellion. Cuba had long been of concern to U.S. diplomats. Only Cuba and neighboring Puerto Rico had survived the breakup of Spain's New World empire in the first quarter of the 19th century. Since 1825, Americans had bent their Caribbean policy toward preventing Spain from selling or surrendering Cuba to another European power.

As early as 1848, President James K. Polk proposed to buy Cuba, authorizing the U.S. minister in Madrid to make an offer for title to the island. The Spanish government declined. In the 1850s Cuba, with its large population of black slaves, became enmeshed in the deepening American crisis over slavery. In 1851, a group of pro-Southern filibusters (armed invaders operating outside the law) landed in Cuba to try to touch off an insurgency that would overthrow the Spanish and lead to

The Bronze Titan

PARTLY OF AFRICAN DESCENT AND KNOWN FOR THAT reason as the Bronze Titan, Antonio Maceo helped launch the Cuban independence movement in 1895. Perhaps because he challenged colonial Spain's racial codes, the Spanish authorities targeted his forces— mostly African Cubans, lightly armed with rifles and machetes, but expert cavalrymen—for special attention.

Maceo's mounted columns preyed on Cuba's sugar economy, Spain's chief source of income, burning mills, warehouses, and standing crops. Gen. Valeriano Weyler's forces pursued Maceo relentlessly. In early December 1896, Maceo, with around 150 men, approached the town of Mariel, just west of Havana, and prepared to cross its *trocha*—one of a system of fortified belts the Spanish had built to restrict the insurgents' movements.

It was one of Spain's strongest fortifications, brightly lit, and with a garrison of 14,000 men. Maceo shrewdly decided to flank it by sea. Taking 17 men in a small boat, he skirted the *trocha* on the night of December 6. But Weyler's forces caught his detachment in an ambush early on December 7.

Maceo fought back fiercely. "This is going well!" he is reported to have called out, moments before bullets smashed into his face and chest. The insurgents recovered Maceo's corpse from the battlefield afterward and buried it near an abandoned farmhouse along the boundary of Havana and Pinar del Río provinces.

U.S. acquisition of the island. The Spanish captured the entire filibustering party; 50 of the 500 invaders were executed. Southerners continued their campaign to annex the island to the Cotton Kingdom. Northerners opposed any addition to slaveholder power.

The United States professed neutrality during the Ten Years' War, though in New York City the rebel leaders, known collectively as the *Junta,* had operated freely to raise money and organize arms shipments to the island. If anything, American support for Cuban independence had broadened and deepened by 1895. There were mass meetings in New York, Chicago, and other cities. That same year, the American Federation of Labor approved a resolution of support for the insurgents at its national convention. "The revolution is one of the most righteous ever declared in any country and should be supported by every lover of liberty and free government in this country," the *Journal* of the Knights of Labor proclaimed.

America's newspapers were solidly pro-Cuban. The cosmopolitan Martí had been a friend of the influential editor of the *New York Sun*, Charles A. Dana. Even the soldierly Gómez recognized the tremendous power of American journalism. "Without a press, we shall get nowhere," he acknowledged. American veterans' groups, including the Grand Army of the Republic, expressed sympathy for the rebellion.

President Grover Cleveland, meantime, followed a policy of strict neutrality. Despite prodding from Congress, he refused to recognize Cuban belligerency, a formal point of international law that would have allowed American firms to legally sell arms and other supplies to the insurgents. In April 1896, Cleveland offered U.S. aid in mediating the question of autonomy for the Cubans—Home Rule—under Spanish sovereignty. The rebels refused to discuss anything short of full independence. The Spanish, especially General Weyler, still believed they could crush the insurgency.

American newspapers, fed a steady diet of atrocity stories by Cuban press officers in New York, were perhaps the insurrection's most powerful ally. There were more than 40 dailies in New York City alone. Among the most sensational of the city's so-called yellow journals were *The World* of Hungarian-born Joseph Pulitzer and the *New York Journal* of William Randolph Hearst, a Harvard dropout who used his father's wealth to buy his way into the newspaper business.

Appropriately, given their tendency toward exaggeration and even outright invention, the yellow newspapers had taken their nickname from a comic strip, "The Yellow Kid," the first comic to be printed in color. *The World* had the strip first; the *Journal* later lured its creator away with a higher salary. The rivalry between the newspapers spread to their news columns. By 1895, Pulitzer and Hearst were engaged in a deadly circulation war. They used stories of Cuban insurgent heroism and Spanish cruelty—occasionally true, more often fabricated—to boost sales.

The yellow journals saw in "Butcher" Weyler the personification of Spanish evil. Hearst's *Journal* called him "pitiless, cold, an exterminator of men." The *Journal* went on: "There is nothing to prevent his carnal, animal brain from running riot with itself in inventing tortures and infamies of bloody debauchery." In several large American cities, there

William Randolph
Hearst (1863–1951)
(Library of Congress)

were mass rallies and Cuban fairs; in some smaller towns, the citizenry turned out to burn Weyler in effigy.

News organizations sent their star reporters to Cuba and hired well-known popular writers and illustrators to cover the war. The novelist Stephen Crane, whose *The Red Badge of Courage* (1895) imaginatively recreated the Civil War battle of Chancellorsville, went to the island in early 1897 to report the conflict from the Cuban rebels' side. Hearst sent Richard Harding Davis and the artist Frederic Remington, who was already famous for his paintings of cowboys, Indians, and soldiers. Hearst paid Davis the princely salary of $3,000 a month to report the story for the *Journal.* Wrote Davis, in a fair approximation of impartiality unusual in 1896–97:

> I always imagined that houses were destroyed during a war because they got in the way of cannon balls or they were burned because they might offer shelter to the enemy, but here they are destroyed with the purpose of making the war horrible and hurrying up the end. The insurgents began first by destroying the sugar mills, some of which were worth millions of dollars in machinery, and now the Spaniards

are burning the homes of the people and herding them in around the towns to starve out the insurgents. So all day long wherever you look you see great heavy columns of smoke rising into this beautiful sky above the magnificent palms.

More typical was Davis's report of three young, attractive Cuban women being subjected to a strip search aboard the U.S. steamer *Olivette* in Havana harbor. Remington's illustration showed three rough-looking Spanish policemen leering at a naked girl. The women, embarrassed by the *Journal*'s account, swiftly set the record straight: Women officials had searched them in a private room, far from the eyes of Spanish males.

The New Navy

AT THE END OF THE CIVIL WAR IN 1865, THE UNITED States maintained the largest and most powerful navy in the world, with more than 700 vessels. By 1880, it had shrunk to the 12th largest. Only 70 steam-powered warships flew the Stars and Stripes.

Lobbyists for a strong navy prodded Congress to action in the 1880s. The first ships of the "new navy," steel-hulled and lightly armored, or "protected," cruisers of the *Atlanta* class, joined the fleet in the middle years of the decade. In September 1888 Congress adopted the largest naval budget since the Civil War, $16 million, to fund construction of the armored cruiser *New York,* the protected cruiser *Olympia,* and five other vessels.

Naval construction accelerated in the 1890s as the United States began to look beyond its shores for economic expansion. Imperial rivalries—confrontations with Britain over Venezuela, with Germany over Samoa, and with Chile over mob attacks on American sailors—seemed to make the acquisition of a blue-water fleet a national necessity.

When Congress appropriated funds to build three armored battleships, the modernization of the navy was well underway. They were powerful vessels, armed with four 13-inch turret guns and eight eight-inch guns capable of piercing an adversary's steel armor at long range. One of the three, the USS *Oregon,* commissioned in 1896, would make an epic voyage from California around Cape Horn in 1898, reaching Cuba in time for the decisive sea battle of Santiago.

Remington soon wearied of Havana's café life. He is alleged to have cabled Hearst for permission to return to New York. "Everything is quiet," the cable supposedly claimed. "There is no trouble. There will be no war." According to legend, Hearst answered: "Please remain. You furnish the pictures and I'll furnish the war."

Hearst always denied the story. Still, his paper stepped up its demands for U.S. action. Congress continued to press for recognition of Cuban independence, and even for outright U.S. intervention. President Cleveland resisted these calls. He enforced U.S. neutrality by ordering the customs and revenue services to break up filibustering expeditions and intercept arms shipments. To decrease the likelihood of incidents, he stopped U.S. Navy courtesy calls to Cuban ports and directed the North Atlantic Squadron to shift its winter exercises from the Caribbean to the colder seas off the Virginia Capes.

In early 1897 Cleveland, a Democrat who had not sought reelection, prepared to transfer power to the Republican William McKinley, who had been elected the previous November. McKinley told the outgoing president he hoped to be as effective as Cleveland had been in preserving the peace.

Still, pressures were mounting on both sides. In Madrid, Spanish leaders faced political difficulties of their own that seemed to make a peaceful settlement unlikely. American support for the *insurrectos* had inflamed opinion in Spain. There had been anti-American demonstrations in the capital; a mob in Barcelona had stoned the U.S. consulate there. In any case, Weyler had been no more successful than Campos in quelling the rebellion. The Liberal opposition began to distance itself from the Cuban policies of the Conservative prime minister, Antonio Cánovas del Castillo.

In turn, Cánovas worried that any compromise over Cuba would provoke a right-wing backlash that could threaten the existence of the Spanish monarchy. (A queen regent, María Cristina, ruled on behalf of her son Alfonso XIII, who would not come of age until 1902.) There were financial embarrassments, too. The cost of fighting the insurgency had nearly bankrupted the government treasury.

An anarchist shot and killed Cánovas in August 1897, a murder that had the unforeseen effect of jolting Spain into a new policy for Cuba. The Liberal leader, Práxedes Sagasta, succeeded Cánovas. "After having sent out 200,000 men and poured out so great a quantity of blood, we are masters of no other territory in the island save that upon which our

Founder of the American Red Cross Clara Barton traveled to Cuba to provide aid in 1898. *(Library of Congress, Prints & Photographs Division [LC-USZ62-113045])*

soldiers stand," he had said a few months before. "We have ruin, desolation and misery in the four provinces of Cuba."

Sagasta acted immediately upon taking power. He recalled Weyler and offered Cuba complete autonomy but still under the Spanish flag. Weyler's successor as captain general, Ramón Blanco, took steps to ease the plight of the *reconcentrados,* though he did not actually suspend the policy. He also gave Clara Barton of the American Red Cross permission to begin distributing relief on the island.

The insurgents rejected home rule, but the rebel leaders were often at cross purposes, beset by political disagreements and racial enmity. Conservative white leaders feared that black Cubans would come to dominate the movement. The death of the charismatic Maceo in December 1896 had lessened those fears, though Spanish propagandists persisted in raising the specter of a black republic. Civilian and military leaders continued to clash over policy, methods and control. The rebels did, however, agree on one essential point: There would be no peace before independence.

The right-wing backlash that Cánovas had dreaded did occur, though not in Madrid. Several dozen Spanish Army officers led mobs of *peninsulares* through the streets of Havana on January 12, 1898, in protest against the Sagasta government's offer of autonomy. The mobs sacked the premises of four newspapers that had spoken out for Home Rule. The outburst was mild as such things sometimes went, but it had one fateful result. Within two weeks, the battleship *Maine* dropped anchor in Havana Harbor.

2
OUTBREAK

Only the *Maine*'s masts and twisted forward parts were visible as day broke on February 16, 1898. The other ships in Havana Harbor flew their flags at half-mast in sympathy, a small comfort, perhaps, for Capt. Charles Sigsbee. The U.S. lighthouse tender *Fern* arrived from Key West to survey the wreck. An American naval inquiry board prepared to assemble in Havana to try to determine what had caused the explosion.

As the initial shock wore off, the political implications became clearer. "Gather every fact you can to prove the *Maine* catastrophe cannot be attributed to us," the Madrid authorities cabled Captain General Ramón Blanco in Havana. In Washington, Navy Secretary John Long noted in his diary that a man's political bias shaped his opinion of the cause of the sinking. "If he is a conservative he is sure that it was an accident," Long wrote; "if he is a jingo, he is equally sure that it was by design."

The U.S. Navy's leading armaments expert told a Washington newspaper he believed the loss of the *Maine* to have been an accident, most likely the result of a coal bunker fire. This expression of opinion infuriated Long's assistant secretary, Theodore Roosevelt. The term *jingo*, denoting aggressive patriotism, had been coined on a British music hall stage in 1878. It caught Roosevelt's attitude perfectly: He was as threatening and warlike a jingo as could be found in Washington. Roosevelt accused the naval officer, Capt. Philip Alger, of taking the Spanish side.

"All the best men in the Department agree that, whether probable or not, it certainly is *possible* that the ship was blown up by a mine," said Roosevelt, who himself was altogether untroubled by doubt. "The *Maine*

The wreck of the *Maine* in Havana Harbor *(National Archives)*

was sunk by an act of dirty treachery on the part of the Spaniards," he announced.

The newspapers were just as bellicose. "Destruction of the warship *Maine* was the work of an enemy," Hearst's *Journal* concluded on February 17, two days after the explosion. After scanning a week's worth of blaring headlines, E. L. Godkin, editor of the weekly *Nation,* reached this verdict on the behavior of the Hearst and Pulitzer publications: "Nothing so disgraceful has ever been known in the history of journalism." Godkin accused the papers of gross misrepresentation, deliberate invention, wanton recklessness. They were firebrands, he said, tossed into the American crowd in an attempt to ignite a war.

The naval court of inquiry convened on February 21 aboard the tender *Mangrove* in Havana Harbor. Teams of divers went down to inspect the wreck. They worked slowly, groping blindly in the murk and moving awkwardly in the soft ooze of the harbor bottom. One diver, searching Captain Sigsbee's cabin, found the keys to the ammunition magazines. The discovery seemed to rule out sabotage.

Sigsbee and his officers were piped aboard the *Mangrove* for questioning. The captain dismissed the possibility of a coal fire. He told the court the coal stored in the forward bunkers had been inspected before it was taken aboard; that the magazines had been inspected recently and found shipshape; and that the ship's fire alarms were in working order. Though the court met in absolute privacy, U.S. consul Fitzhugh Lee cabled Washington that he believed a mine had sunk the *Maine,* but that the Spanish were not responsible. Perhaps the insurgents, hoping to provoke war, had done it themselves, Lee suggested.

In the White House, President McKinley tried to shut out the roar of the press. "I don't propose to be swept off my feet by the catastrophe," he wrote Indiana senator Charles Fairbanks. "The country can afford to withhold its judgement and not strike an avenging blow until the truth is known." The 25th president, a benevolent, peaceable, and deeply religious Ohioan, had no desire to go to war with Spain. A Civil War veteran of the

William McKinley
(1843–1901)
(Library of Congress)

battles of Antietam and Cedar Creek, he had glimpsed the terrible face of battle. "War should never be entered on until every agency of peace has failed; peace is preferable to war in almost every contingency," McKinley had said in his inaugural address in March 1897.

But there were doubts about the president's forcefulness and the strength of his leadership. "A kindly soul in a spineless body," the historian Samuel Eliot Morison said of him. McKinley would have to resist demands for action while he searched for a peaceful settlement that would appease Spain, satisfy the Cubans and still the clamor of the yellow journals. The furor over the *Maine* disaster certainly complicated McKinley's task, as did Americans' genuine concern for the tragedy of the Cuban rebellion.

Other forces buffeted McKinley too, not least the changing attitudes of Americans toward the world beyond the seas. These ranged from an unabashed lust for money to the mystical claims of a higher, sterner duty. "Free Cuba would mean a great market for the United States; it would mean an opportunity for American capital; it would mean an opportunity for the development of that splendid island," said Massachusetts senator Henry Cabot Lodge. His close friend Roosevelt lifted his bespectacled eyes toward misty heights of national glory to be stormed and seized. "There are higher things in life than the soft and easy enjoyment of material comfort," Roosevelt declared in an 1897 speech. "It is through strife, or the readiness for strife, that a nation must win greatness. No national life is worth having if the nation is not willing, when the need shall arise, to stake everything on the supreme arbitrament of war."

In 1890, the historian Frederick Jackson Turner noted, the U.S. Census Bureau had announced the closing of the American frontier. For decades the West had been the outlet for American restlessness and ambition. "American energy will continually demand a wider field for its exercise," Turner wrote. For Lodge, Roosevelt and others now bearing the label "imperialists," overseas expansion became the cry. "Whether they will or no, Americans must begin to look outward," wrote Alfred Thayer Mahan, the naval strategist whose book *The Influence of Sea Power upon History* (1890) deeply influenced the thinking of these imperialists.

A former president of the U.S. Naval War College in Newport, Rhode Island, Mahan argued that America's future as an industrial power depended on foreign markets for American products. Only sea power could guarantee access to distant markets in competition with other

Naval historian Alfred Thayer Mahan advocated expansion of U.S. sea power. *(Library of Congress, Prints & Photographs Division [LC-USZ62-120219])*

maritime nations. America, Mahan concluded, must have a large, modern fleet, a canal linking the Caribbean and the Pacific, and overseas colonies—such as those the Spanish possessed—for bases and coaling stations to serve the warships.

Roosevelt had dabbled in naval history; the great Mahan himself had spoken kindly of Roosevelt's book *The Naval War of 1812.* When he became assistant secretary of the navy, Roosevelt found himself in a position to convert his ideas into action. By the autumn of 1897 he had caught the president's attention. In a series of private meetings, Roosevelt lobbied McKinley for aggressive action against the Spanish.

"I gave him a paper showing exactly where all our ships are, and I also sketched in outline what I thought ought to be done if things looked menacing about Spain, urging the necessity of taking an immediate and prompt initiative if we wished to avoid the chance of some serious trouble," Roosevelt wrote, recalling one of his sessions with the president.

The Spanish, as Roosevelt doubtless knew, were in no condition to go over to the offensive. Shortly after taking office in Madrid, Premier Sagasta received a confidential report on conditions in Cuba. In summary, it read:

The administration has reached the last stage of disarray and disorder; the army, exhausted and bloodless, filling the hospitals, without the power to fight or hardly even to lift their arms; more than three hundred thousand *concentrados* suffering or starving, dying of hunger and misery all around the towns; the people frightened, in the grip of real terror, obliged to abandon their homes and properties in order to suffer under even more terrible tyranny, with no opportunity to escape this fearful situation except by going and joining the ranks of the rebels.

The Cuban insurgents were scarcely in better shape. The spoils of an August 1897 victory at Las Tunas only served to emphasize the extent of their needs. Overrunning the fortified town, they captured 1,000 rifles, 1 million rounds of ammunition and 10 wagonloads of medicines. Yet food remained scarce. Frederick Funston, an American adventurer fighting with the Cubans, suffered from constant, gnawing hunger. "Pack trains scoured the country, taking from the miserable people the last sweet potato, ear of corn or banana that could be found," Funston recalled. There was never enough. The *insurrectos,* half-starved, sickly, and in tatters, stumbled on, fighting as best they could what seemed to be an endless war.

In Havana, Clara Barton labored to bring aid to the suffering Cubans. The Sagasta government in Madrid had given her permission, through Captain-General Blanco, to distribute food, medicine, and other comforts among the internees, but Spanish local authority, often uncooperative and always corrupt, made a difficult task nearly impossible. She appealed to U.S. consul Lee, with small result. "Every time we try to talk to him, he is in a great hurry, is always very busy & yet he seems to find plenty of time to devote to his large circle of lady friends here," one of Barton's Red Cross assistants complained. Consul Lee spoke no Spanish, and anyway the colonial officials were suspicious of his ties with American businessmen and wealthy Cubans who favored U.S. intervention (he hoped to make a fortune for himself from investments in the Havana streetcar system).

U.S. troops arriving in Cuba found victims of starvation like these in Matanzas. *(Library of Congress, Prints & Photographs Division [LC-USZ62-75981])*

Those pressing for an expanded U.S. role found support from an unlikely source, Senator Redfield Proctor. A conservative Republican from Vermont, Proctor had shown little interest in taking up the cause of Cuban independence. But a brief visit to the island in March 1898 converted him into an interventionist. Conditions there appalled him. "To me," Proctor said on his return to Washington, "the strongest appeal is not the barbarity practiced by Weyler, nor the loss of the *Maine*, but the spectacle of a million and a half people, the entire native population of Cuba, struggling for freedom and deliverance from the worst misgovernment of which I have ever had knowledge."

The speech failed to move Thomas Reed, the Speaker of the House of Representatives, who opposed U.S. adventuring abroad. Reed noted that Proctor had made a fortune out of marble. "A war will make a large market for gravestones," he remarked acidly. But public opinion had left Reed and other conservatives far behind. The *Wall Street Journal*

"A Message to Garcia"

WITH WAR IMMINENT, U.S. PLANNERS SOUGHT THE latest information from Cuba. Lt. Andrew Rowan first made contact with Cuban *insurrectos* in Jamaica, then landed at night on the coast of Cuba. After making his way through the Spanish lines to the camp of insurgent leader Calixto García, Rowan returned safely with important maps and details on insurgent operations and Spanish troop concentrations.

In February 1899, the writer and crafts communitarian Elbert Hubbard memorialized this dangerous if rather routine soldierly exploit in an inaccurate but stirring essay titled "A Message to Garcia." It made García's name one of the most famous of the Spanish-American War, and it became one of the best-selling business motivational pieces of all time.

Hubbard himself called the essay "a literary trifle" and claimed he had it written in an hour after dinner. In his version, Rowan landed from an open boat and made his way alone through miles of treacherous jungle with a message from President McKinley in an oilskin pouch strapped to his chest.

Wrote Hubbard, "By the eternal! There is a man whose form should be cast in deathless bronze and the statue placed in every college in the land. It is not book-learning young men need, nor instruction about this or that, but a stiffening of the vertebrae which will cause them to be loyal to a trust, to act promptly, concentrate their energies; do the thing—'carry a message to Garcia!'"

Hubbard published the essay in his crafts community monthly *The Philistine.* The president of the New York Central Railroad read it there and sought permission to reprint 500,000 copies. Eventually 40 million copies of this exotic blend of adventure story and motivational business primer were distributed.

reported that Proctor's speech persuaded many business leaders, heretofore skeptical, that the United States ought to intervene in Cuba.

The interventionists were beginning to sway McKinley. As early as March 6, he ordered the Navy Department's ordnance bureau, the agency responsible for fitting out the fleet with guns and ammunition, to shift to a war footing. Three days later, Congress approved a $50 million appropriation for national defense. One congressman, the former

Confederate cavalry general Joseph Wheeler, celebrated the measure with a piercing rebel yell. The money came from the U.S. Treasury surplus, a detail that did not escape Sagasta's nearly bankrupt government. "It has not excited the Spaniards," Stewart Woodford, the U.S. minister to Spain, said of the appropriation. "It has stunned them." Sixty percent of the money went to the navy, which used the windfall to buy auxiliary vessels and to stockpile supplies of coal, ammunition, and other war matériel.

The president, meantime, awaited the court of inquiry's report on the *Maine* disaster. The court signed its findings on March 21 and sent them north to Washington by special courier. McKinley and his cabinet reviewed the report on March 25, a Friday, but decided to withhold it from Congress until the following Monday, in order to allow more time for negotiations. The Associated Press news service managed to obtain an accurate summary of the findings during the weekend, however, and papers all across America carried the story in their Monday morning editions.

The court determined there had been two explosions: the first a mine under the keel of the *Maine;* the second, touched off by the initial blast, in an ammunition magazine in the forward part of the ship. The court did not, however, fix responsibility for the planting of the mine. Captain Sigsbee, testifying on March 31 before the Senate Foreign Relations Committee, said he thought a mine detonated electrically from the shore had blown up the *Maine.* He implied that the Spanish were to blame. Still, Sigsbee could not explain why no wires had been found, nor any evidence of a control station ashore. Later inquiry challenged the court's findings, though the cause of the disaster remained a mystery. (In the mid-1970s Adm. Hyman G. Rickover, a distinguished U.S. naval officer, concluded after an exhaustive technical analysis that spontaneous combustion of bunker coal had touched off the explosion. "There is no evidence that a mine destroyed the *Maine,*" Rickover said.)

There was little reason in 1898 to question the naval board's verdict. The United States used it to increase diplomatic pressure on Spain. The day after the report became public, American ambassador Woodford in Madrid delivered an ultimatum demanding the revocation of *reconcentración* and an immediate armistice. Under prodding from Congress, McKinley escalated the demand: full independence for Cuba and a complete withdrawal of Spanish power from the island. The Spanish

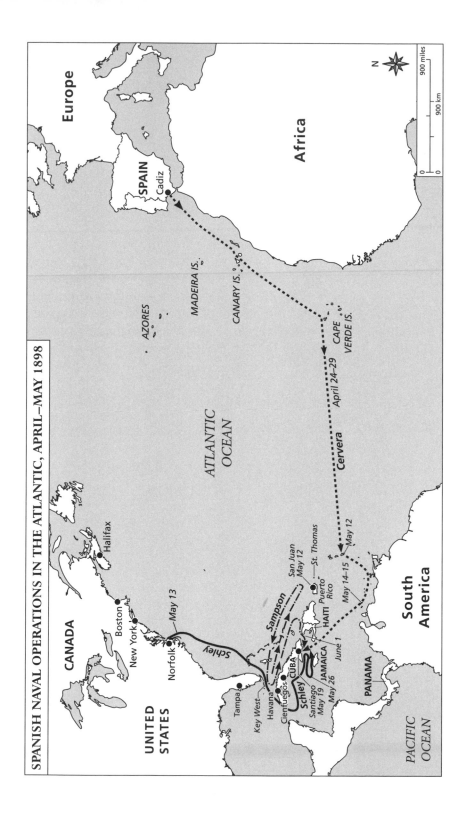

SPANISH NAVAL OPERATIONS IN THE ATLANTIC, APRIL–MAY 1898

N

0   900 miles
0   900 km

Europe

SPAIN
Cadiz

Africa

MADEIRA IS.

AZORES

CANARY IS.

CAPE
VERDE IS.

April 24–29

Cervera

ATLANTIC
OCEAN

CANADA

Halifax

Boston

New York

May 13

Norfolk

UNITED
STATES

Tampa

Key West

Havana

Cienfuegos

Schley

Santiago
May 19

May 26

CUBA

JAMAICA

Schley

Sampson

San Juan
May 12

St. Thomas

Puerto
Rico

May 14–15

May 12

HAITI

June 1

PANAMA

South
America

PACIFIC
OCEAN

government offered to rescind the *reconcentración* policy and to grant a cease-fire at the insurgents' request. A few days later, Madrid agreed to initiate an armistice. But the concessions were too little, too late.

"There is no stopping place short of the absolute independence of Cuba," the *New York Times* wrote in the wake of the *Maine* report. "It would have been as easy to end the War of the Revolution at Bunker Hill or the Civil War at Bull Run as to turn back now."

McKinley submitted the question to Congress on Monday, April 11. While the senators and representatives deliberated, Assistant Secretary of the Navy Roosevelt fretted. He wanted action. Roosevelt filled his diary with fiery entries expressing unbridled contempt for anyone reluctant to make immediate war. "The President still feebly is painfully trying for peace," he wrote on April 16. "His weakness and vacillation are even more ludicrous than painful." To Roosevelt's relief, on April 19 the House and Senate passed joint resolutions that recognized Cuban independence, demanded Spanish withdrawal and granted the president authority to use military and naval forces to end the war on the island.

The Spanish were pushed to the wall. Appeals to the European powers were unavailing. "It would be acting disloyally if I allowed Your Excellency to believe there was any real prospect of active intervention by the powers in Spain's favor," the German foreign minister wrote the Spanish ambassador to Berlin. "I admire the courage Spain has shown, but I would admire more a display of plain practical sense." Spain, clearly, had no choice but to back down or fight. If the continental powers were neutral, however, the British were openly pro-American. The American ambassador in London believed the British would even offer the assistance of the Royal Navy should the United States require it.

McKinley signed the congressional resolutions on April 20. The State Department sent an ultimatum to Spain. Diplomatic relations were broken off on April 21, and McKinley ordered a naval blockade of Cuban ports. The U.S. North Atlantic Squadron—the battleships *Iowa* and *Indiana*, the armored cruiser *New York*, three light cruisers, and escort vessels—arrived off Havana the afternoon of April 22.

These initial moves were in accord with the navy's war plan for Cuba, which had been developed at the Naval War College. The plan called for the blockade, together with troop landings in Cuba and Puerto Rico, before the Spanish could ferry reinforcements across the Atlantic. It also proposed an attack on Spanish forces at Manila, in the Philippine Islands in the far Pacific.

A Mismatch of Powers

HEAVILY IN DEBT, AND WITH LITTLE CREDIT AVAILABLE for arms purchases, Spain could not afford to match America's military buildup as tensions over Cuba heightened. The Caribbean lay 3,000 miles distant from Spain's main naval port, Cádiz, but the Spanish admirals hardly seem to have considered how their warships would get there, or what they could accomplish once they arrived.

"Not the least preparation was made, either on land or on the sea," wrote Victor Concas y Palau, captain of the cruiser *Maria Teresa,* "while the whole world was under the impression that we were frantically getting ready for a struggle to the bitter end."

Spain had no battleships ready for sea in April 1898 and only four armored cruisers—the newest of which, *Cristóbal Colón,* carried wooden dummies in place of the yet to be delivered 10-inch main battery. And only 11 light craft—destroyers, torpedo boats, gunboats—were fit for service on the eve of war with the United States.

True, Spain did maintain 196,000 troops in Cuba and 51,000 in the Philippines. But the forces in Cuba were widely scattered, bled down, and demoralized after years of inconclusive fighting against the insurgents, and they were woefully unprepared to offer battle to a modern expeditionary force. Nor were Cuba's transportation systems set up for the rapid movement of troops to meet invaders where they came ashore.

All the same, Spain's leaders believed they had no choice but to go to war. There were fears of a right-wing coup at home should the Spanish government be seen to be caving in to American pressure. Besides, many of the Spanish assumed, as U.S. ambassador Stewart Woodford said, "that the [Cuban] rebellion only lives because of [U.S.] sympathy and assistance." In the end, Spain proved willing to accept war rather than face a political crisis at home.

The U.S. Navy, with more than 100 vessels of all types and 13,000 well-trained officers and men, found itself amply prepared to carry out the plan. Four first-class battleships formed the main striking arm of the fleet. One of these, the USS *Oregon,* based in San Francisco, had set out on March 16 on a 16,000-mile voyage around Cape Horn, bound for the Caribbean. (Imperialists cited this long roundabout, which would take 67 days, as a further argument for a Central American canal.)

The 12,000-ton battleship, armed with four 13-inch turret guns and a secondary battery of eight eight-inch guns and girded at the waterline with an 18-inch-thick belt of armor, would be a powerful addition to the American naval forces off Cuba.

Richard Harding Davis, Hearst's celebrity reporter, observed the blockade firsthand from the *New York,* the flagship of the North Atlantic Squadron. The clockwork efficiency of the ship's crew impressed him deeply. He did, however, find life aboard what he termed a "floating monastery" a trifle tame. Blockade work struck him as dull. Davis wrote:

> It was very difficult to believe we were at war. A peaceful blockade does not lend itself to that illusion. From the deck of the *New York,* we overlooked the coast of Cuba as from the roof of a high building; and all that we saw of the war was a peaceful panorama of mountain-ranges and yellow villages, royal palms and tiny forts, like section-houses along the line of a railroad, and in the distance Morro Castle and the besieged city of Havana basking in a haze of glaring sunlight.

Congress approved a formal declaration of war on April 25, retroactive to April 21, the day McKinley ordered the blockade. The president issued a call for 125,000 volunteers to supplement the 28,000-man regular army. Tens of thousands of young men crowded into the recruiting offices. Theodore Roosevelt paced his office at the Navy Department, scheming for an officer's commission in the First U.S. Volunteer Cavalry—soon to become famous as the Rough Riders. Frank James of the notorious outlaw family volunteered to lead a company of cowboys and associated Wild West toughs against the Spanish.

Fitzhugh Lee had left his consul's post in Havana on April 10. He would be given a major general's commission and a senior command in the Cuban expeditionary force. Another elderly former Confederate cavalryman, Joe Wheeler, the Alabama congressman, would also become a major general. Such developments inspired flights of patriotic oratory, hymns to the final sealing of the old Civil War divisions. "The blue and the gray shall be blended into one vast army, flying the banner of freedom, keeping step to the heartbeat of humanity, and moving up on the last contingency of despotism," said Representative Henry F. Thomas of Michigan.

A cartoonist contrasts a jingo with a cool-headed, fair-minded American: Congress voted a formal declaration of war on April 25, 1898. *(National Archives)*

OUTBREAK

Half a world away in Hong Kong, Commodore George Dewey prepared to take the U.S. Asiatic Squadron to sea. John Long, the navy secretary, had alerted him in early April that war seemed imminent. With the formal declaration, rules of neutrality required the squadron to leave British Hong Kong. At the far end of the long transpacific communications cable, Dewey anxiously awaited word to steam for Philippine waters and a rendezvous with the Spanish fleet.

3

"YOU MAY FIRE . . ."

President McKinley admitted having to search the globe for the Philippines. "I could not have told where those darned islands were within two thousand miles," he said. Over at the Navy Department, Assistant Secretary Theodore Roosevelt could have given McKinley all the information he required. Taking the initiative while in temporary charge of the department, Roosevelt in February had ordered Commodore George Dewey to be prepared, in the event of war with Spain, to attack Manila.

Operating behind the scenes, Roosevelt had helped to engineer Dewey's appointment to the Pacific command. Roosevelt admired him as a capable, decisive officer who would not hesitate to act on his own responsibility. Vermont-born, an 1858 Naval Academy graduate, Dewey had served in Adm. David Farragut's Mississippi River fleet during the Civil War, taking part in the capture of New Orleans in April 1862. Later in the war, he saw blockade service in the Atlantic.

Dewey advanced steadily if slowly in the peacetime navy, rising to commander in 1872, to captain in 1884, and to commodore in 1896. Command of the Asiatic Squadron normally carried rear admiral's rank. For some reason, possibly resentment in the navy of the political influence exerted on his behalf, promotion did not come Dewey's way when he hoisted his flag on the USS *Olympia* at Nagasaki, Japan, in January 1898. The flag bore a commodore's single star.

Seven ships formed Dewey's Asiatic Squadron: *Olympia* and three other armored cruisers, *Raleigh, Baltimore,* and *Boston;* two gunboats, *Petrel* and *Concord;* and the revenue cutter *McCulloch.* Dewey ordered the ships into their gray war paint, bought two coal-carrying transports,

Adm. George Dewey
aboard his flagship,
the USS *Olympia*
(National Archives)

and sent the *Baltimore* into drydock to have her bottom plates scraped
and repaired. By March, he had taken the squadron to Hong Kong, the
British-ruled trading island off the China coast only 600 miles from
Manila.

Like their president, Americans knew almost nothing of the Philippines, an archipelago of 7,000 tropical islands in the southwest Pacific.
The Spanish explorer Ferdinand Magellan visited the islands in 1521.
They were named for King Philip II; by the 1560s, the Spanish had
nearly completed the conquest. Manila, on the large island of Luzon,
developed into a leading commercial center of the Far East. Still, U.S.
naval intelligence maintained so small a file on the place that Commodore Dewey had to buy charts of Manila Bay from a Hong Kong
ship's chandlery.

On the outbreak of war, the British authorities advised Dewey that
his warships must leave Hong Kong. Formal neutrality, however, did
not prevent the British from taking part in the send-off. "As the
Olympia passed the English hospital ships, they gave us three hearty
cheers," a sailor recalled. "Three steam launches filled with enthusiastic
Americans followed us down the harbor, waving flags and wishing us

Roosevelt and His Boss

IN THEODORE ROOSEVELT'S JUDGMENT, NAVY SECRETARY John Long too often failed to rise to the historic occasion. Roosevelt, the assistant secretary, found his superior indecisive, inattentive to detail, and lacking in expertise on naval matters. And it was true that Long, a former Massachusetts governor and a political ally of President William McKinley, had no special aptitude for his job. So often was he absent from the office on vacation during the summer months that Roosevelt began to think of himself as the "hot-weather secretary."

During Long's absence in September 1897, Roosevelt engineered the appointment of Commodore George Dewey as commander of the U.S. Asiatic Squadron. Should war with Spain come, Roosevelt wanted a bold officer in charge, one unafraid to act on his own, and he suspected that Long would favor a more timid commander. "I've looked into his eyes," Roosevelt said of Dewey. "He's a fighter."

In February 1898, with tensions with Spain on the rise over Cuba, Dewey in his flagship USS *Olympia* sailed from Japan for British Hong Kong, only 600 miles distant from Manila, the Philippine capital. The day after he arrived, he received word of the destruction of the USS *Maine* in Havana Harbor. Then Roosevelt—again with Long away from his desk at the Navy Department—ordered the rest of the Asiatic Squadron to join Dewey in Hong Kong, and he flashed orders for two warships to sail at once for the China coast to reinforce him.

Meantime, Roosevelt impressed the critical importance of Spain's Philippine possessions upon Long. With a strong push from Roosevelt, Long Urged McKinley to authorize Dewey to descend on Manila. The orders reached Dewey on April 27, eight days after Congress authorized military action against Spain.

"Long is at last awake," Roosevelt confided to his diary. "I have the Navy on good shape."

God-speed." The squadron steamed to Mirs Bay, a quiet anchorage 30 miles north of Hong Kong, to await orders. Dewey passed word for the ships to clear for action. Sailors removed hatches, chests, paneling, and other wooden objects that could splinter or burn and stored them in the transports.

McKinley authorized the attack on Manila Bay on April 24. Navy Secretary John Long cabled to Dewey: "Commence operations at once, particularly against Spanish fleet. You must capture vessels or destroy. Use utmost endeavors." The Asiatic Squadron, carrying 1,700 officers and men and three newspaper correspondents, weighed anchor and stood out from Mirs Bay into the China Sea on the afternoon of April 27.

The seven warships steamed slowly, at eight knots, so that the heavily laden transports could keep up. Dewey expected to encounter strong coastal defenses, particularly at the fortress of Corregidor Island at the entrance to Manila Bay. The channel leading to the city of Manila would probably be mined. There were the Spanish warships too, six old, outdated vessels, as it turned out: the cruisers *Reina Cristina* and *Castilla* (the latter built of wood) and four smaller cruisers. Collectively, Dewey's ships carried 53 guns ranging up to eight inches in caliber. The Spanish mounted only 31 big guns altogether, none larger than 6.3 inches.

The Spanish, at any rate, knew the Americans were coming. The captain-general of the islands issued a stirring proclamation to that effect:

> A squadron manned by foreigners, possessing neither instruction nor discipline, is preparing to come to this archipelago with the ruffianly intention of robbing us of all that means life, honor, and liberty, to treat you as tribes refractory to civilization, to take possession of your riches. Vain designs! Ridiculous boastings!

A dispatch vessel brought Dewey a copy of the proclamation. He ordered the broadside read aloud to his crews, who chose to treat its threats as comedy. Still, some of the laughter may have been forced. No one in the squadron knew what to expect. In Hong Kong, British naval officers had rated Spanish fighting qualities highly, and British views always carried weight.

Dewey's lookouts sighted the coast of Luzon before dawn on April 30. The squadron turned south toward Subic Bay, steaming slowly three or four miles offshore. Dewey had guessed that the Spanish squadron might choose to fight in Subic Bay, an inlet with strong natural defenses. But his scout vessels found Subic deserted. Before proceeding southward, Dewey called the captains aboard the *Olympia* for a conference. He told them the squadron would run past the shore batteries at Corregidor and search out the Spanish fleet in Manila Bay.

Darkness fell. The ships steamed in line astern, the *Olympia* in the vanguard. "Aside from one light at the very stern of each ship, intended as a guide for the next in line, not a glimmer was to be seen aboard any craft in the fleet," wrote the *New York Herald*'s Joseph Stickney in the flagship. "As I looked astern, I could just get a faint suggestion of a ghostly shape where the *Baltimore* grimly held her course." Dewey ordered the men to their guns at 9:45 P.M. The *Olympia* approached Corregidor at 30 minutes before midnight, steering for the broad channel to the south of the island fortress.

Soot in the funnel of the *McCulloch* caught fire, briefly illuminating the squadron in an eerie glare. A Spanish mainland battery fired once or twice, but Corregidor remained unaccountably dark and silent. Soon Dewey's vessels were safely past and on a course for Manila 25 miles distant, steaming at four knots to time their arrival off the city for daybreak on May 1. At four o'clock the commodore ordered coffee and a cold breakfast served to the crews. By first light, the *Olympia* stood within a mile of the Manila waterfront. Lt. C. G. Calkins, the flagship's navigator, counted 16 merchant vessels in the harbor, but no Spanish warships. Then, in the growing light, a lookout sighted the enemy squadron at anchor five miles to the south, at the Cavite naval station.

The Spanish admiral, Patricio Montojo y Pasarón, had planned at first to offer battle in the deep waters of Subic Bay. Montojo actually took the squadron to Subic, but changed his mind after inspecting the unfinished land defenses there. He ordered a return to Manila, reasoning that if his ships were to be sunk, he preferred the shallow waters off the Cavite arsenal. "What a strange conclusion for a naval officer," Dewey remarked afterward.

The American cruisers advanced in close battle order, *Olympia* still in the lead. The Manila shore batteries opened fire as the squadron passed. A shell struck the water close to the *Petrel*, drenching Lt. Bradley A. Fiske at his range-finding post 45 feet above the waterline. Fiske recalled:

> To the south, the land was lower; and there, standing out in clear relief against the bright blue sky, were the awe-inspiring forms of the ships of the Spanish fleet. The *Olympia* turned to the right and headed toward them. The *Baltimore* followed, and then the *Raleigh*.

Dewey's ships closed at a steady eight knots. Calkins saw a "white cloud with a heart of fire" billow up on the landward side. A shell soared into the sky. "They were ready for us then, and meant to fight," he thought. "But a moment later two harmless fountains sprang up miles ahead of our columns, and it was plain that the defense was flurried." As the Americans drew nearer the Spanish marksmanship improved. At 5:41 A.M., at a range of 5,400 yards, Dewey turned to the *Olympia*'s captain: "You may fire when ready, Gridley."

The *Olympia*'s eight-inch guns opened up, concentrating their fire on the *Castilla* and the *Reina Cristina*, the most powerful of Admiral Montojo's ships. The American line steamed roughly parallel to the Spanish, fired deliberately and then turned 180 degrees and passed along the line a second time. The Spanish flagship, the *Reina Cristina*, took several hits that put some guns out of action and wounded a score of sailors. The *Olympia* turned again and led a third pass down the Spanish line.

Below the decks of the American ships, sweating bluejackets labored furiously to supply powder and shells for the big guns and to keep the boilers stoked. They worked stripped to the skin, except for shoes and underdrawers. "The heat was really fearful," Joel Evans, a gunner in the *Boston*, recalled. "The powder smoke settled down, choking us and half-blinding some." Conditions were more hellish still in the boiler rooms. With hatches battened, the engineers and stokers were confined in an iron cauldron, sealed off from the outside world.

"It was so hot our hair was singed," *Olympia* stoker Charles Twitchell remembered. "The clatter of the engines and the roaring of the furnaces made such a din it seemed one's head would burst." The ship lurched violently each time the big guns fired. "The soot and cinders poured down on us in clouds," Twitchell said. "Now and then a big drop of scalding water would fall on our bare heads. We knew it meant sure death if the *Olympia* got a shot through her anywhere in our vicinity."

Lieutenant Fiske recalled being struck by the calmness of the *Petrel*'s crew. "I had seen many pictures of battles and had expected great excitement," he wrote.

> I did not see any excitement whatever. The men seemed to me to be laboring under an intense strain and to be keyed up to the highest pitch; but to be quiet, and under complete self-control, and to be doing the work of handling the guns and ammunition with that mechanical precision which is the result we all hope to get from drill.

The maneuvering of the other ships in the American battle line, as well as their steady firing, had something of a drill about it, too. Fiske continued:

> To me in my elevated perch the whole thing looked like a performance that had been very carefully rehearsed. The ships went slowly and regularly, seldom or never getting out of their relative positions, and only ceased firing at intervals when the smoke became too thick.

Even through the battle smoke, the Americans could observe the devastating effects of their fire. "Thick billows of burning smoke rose up from the Spanish ships and drifted out over the bay," Calkins wrote. "Yet there was no sign of surrender. The red and yellow flag of Spain still flew above the shattered, burning hulks, and their broadsides flashed defiantly." Despite her injuries the *Reina Cristina* weighed anchor and headed into the bay, as though to attack the *Olympia*. The Americans turned a fierce fire on the flagship and drove it inshore. A few moments later, Montojo gave the order to scuttle the ship before the magazines

U.S. warships pour fire into a listing Spanish cruiser, Manila Bay, May 1, 1898. *(U.S. Army Military History Institute)*

movement. At first, anyway, Dewey viewed him as a use-
nerican warship carried Aguinaldo from Hong Kong to
the third week in May. With the commodore's permis-
insurgent headquarters at Cavite. Dewey also supplied
h arms and ammunition for a landward advance on

n, however, shortly instructed Dewey to avoid any com-
Aguinaldo and the insurgents. The islands, the McKinley
suggested, were to be treated as spoils of war. To Wash-
eemed ripe for the taking.

blew up. "When she was raised from her muddy bed five years later," Dewey would write in his autobiography, "eighty skeletons were found in the sickbay."

Still, the commodore could not yet be certain of his victory. Someone reported to him that the squadron's ammunition supplies were running low. At 7:35 A.M., not quite two hours after the opening of the battle, Dewey ordered a pause. As the smoke began to lift, he could begin to assess the results of the five passes his cruisers had made down the Spanish line. "It was clear to me we did not need a very large supply to finish our morning's task," he wrote. The squadron drifted just beyond range of the shore batteries and rested.

During the break, Dewey ordered a second breakfast for the crews and called the captains to the *Olympia* for another conference. Hatches were opened and the men below decks were allowed topside for air. Calkins remembered the breakfast: "There were sardines, corned beef, and hardtack on a corner of the wardroom table, still encumbered by the surgeons' ghastly gear, which was all unstained, however." Indeed, American casualties had been astonishingly light: none killed, only six wounded, all aboard the *Baltimore*.

Afterward, American veterans of the battle looked back in wonder at the outcome. It was as though they had fought under some protective charm. "Under the miraculous providence which ordered the events of that day those six American ships steamed back and forth unharmed for nearly three hours," an officer of the *Baltimore* wrote. But Providence had shown little mercy to the Spanish. Nearly 400 Spanish sailors were killed or wounded.

The *Reina Cristina* had been battered to death and the *Castilla*'s guns were almost silent. The other ships were trapped in the little harbor at the Cavite arsenal. Still, the Spanish had not given up. At 11:15, Dewey signaled for a renewal of the action. The squadron concentrated its full attention on the cruiser *Don Antonio de Ulloa*. The luckless *Ulloa* shortly rolled over and sank in the shallow water of Cavite inlet.

The U.S. gunboat *Petrel* steamed into Cavite harbor and fired several shots. One by one, the flags were hauled down on the surviving Spanish vessels. The *Petrel* sent crews aboard to take formal possession, and then set each ship afire to complete the destruction. At about 12:30 P.M., the gunboat signalled the *Olympia:* "The enemy has surrendered." In a morning's work, the Asiatic Squadron had wrecked 10 Spanish vessels and captured the Cavite naval yard.

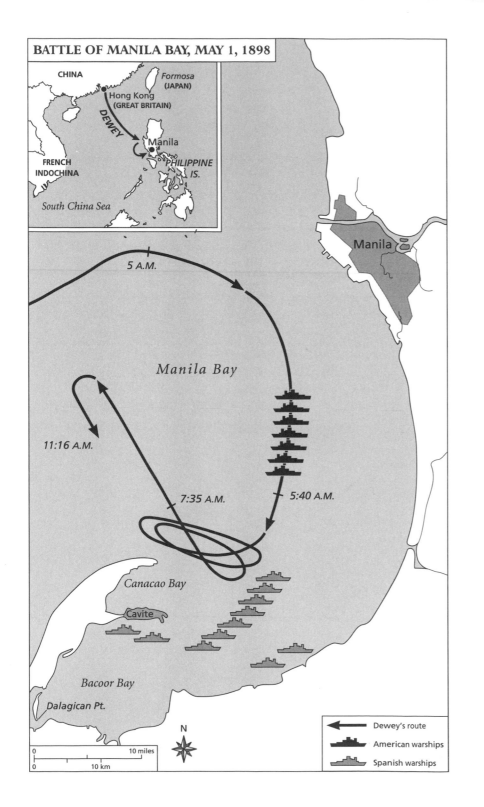

BATTLE OF MANILA BAY, MAY 1, 1898

CHINA

Formosa (JAPAN)

Hong Kong (GREAT BRITAIN)

DEWEY

Manila

FRENCH INDOCHINA

PHILIPPINE IS.

South China Sea

Manila

5 A.M.

Manila Bay

11:16 A.M.

7:35 A.M.

5:40 A.M.

Canacao Bay

Cavite

Bacoor Bay

Dalagican Pt.

N

0   10 miles
0   10 km

→ Dewey's route

American warships

Spanish warships

"Y

Dewey took the victori
Manila waterfront. When t
permission to use the cable
ordered it dredged up from
Spanish agreed to cease firi
communication with the ou
tle choice. "The city was virt
established a base seven th
occupy indefinitely."

Washington, meantime,
Squadron. A full week pas:
Madrid. A rumor spread that
York *World* correspondent re
cabled the news. "I have jus
American triumph at Manila
was destroyed. None of the A
Dewey's official report reache
modore became an instant na

Dew
Is th
And the *Ma*
In the go

President McKinley decide
for the time being. He direc
expeditionary force in San F
report that he could take Mai
force of 5,000 infantry would t
first group of U.S. transport
Philippines on May 25.

The presence of a persisten
plicated matters for Dewey. Th
Cavite arsenal, Aguinaldo clai
that were challenging Spanish
American crisis seemed to offe
afford to miss.

Aguinaldo would claim lat
the Far East led him to believ

In 1898, 29-
Emilio A
rose as th
of the P
independenc
ment. (
Congres.
Photograph
[LC-USZ6

independence
ful ally. An A
Manila durin
sion, he set u
the rebels w
Manila.

Washingt
mitments to
administratic
ington, they

Dewey's sudden coolness did not deter Aguinaldo, whose forces went over to the offensive in late May. They soon controlled all of Cavite province and were closing in on Manila. Aguinaldo proclaimed Philippine independence on June 12, 1898. Eleven days later, he appointed himself head of the Philippine revolutionary government. By month's end, the first contingent of American infantry had reached Manila.

The seeds of a future imperial conflict had been sown. But at home, thousands of miles away, Americans were giddy with Dewey's success and flushed with war fever. Some, like their president, spun their globes in search of the exotic Philippines. Others, easily alarmed, pored over maps of Spain and the North Atlantic, trying to find the Spanish port city of Cádiz and the Cape Verde island group. The newspapers were reporting that a powerful Spanish squadron had put to sea and might be heading for the densely populated, rich, and practically undefended east coast of the United States.

4

THE WAR FROM MAIN STREET

Neither the formal declaration of war on April 25 nor the rousing newspaper headlines had immediate impact on the lives of most Americans. There was no radio, let alone television; distant events did not affect people as directly as they would a century later. Commodore George Dewey's ships destroyed the Spanish fleet off Manila Bay on May 1, but the news of that event took a full week to reach America. Yet despite the remoteness and, as it would turn out, the brevity of this war of the summer of 1898, it nevertheless made an impression on American society.

There was little likelihood that the Spanish could carry the war to the continental United States. Still, naval experts agreed that the Spanish might make effective use of their warships by launching raids on Atlantic seaboard cities. "The patriotic citizens of the States may well come to rue the day that the meddling finger of Uncle Sam was thrust into the hornet's nest of Cuba," the British naval authority Frederick T. Jane wrote acidly. America's own preeminent sea power strategist, Alfred Thayer Mahan, believed that the Spanish fleet could serve a useful purpose merely by hovering just out of view over the horizon, where it would be "a perpetual menace" to the U.S. Navy, which could not guess when or where a blow might fall.

Speculation about Spanish intentions sent a current of fear running down the American East Coast. When the Spanish Atlantic squadron of Admiral Pascual Cervera y Topete sailed on April 29 from the Cape Verde Islands for an unknown destination, alarmist newspaper headlines blew up. "When she was raised from her muddy bed five years later," Dewey would write in his autobiography, "eighty skeletons were found in the sickbay."

Still, the commodore could not yet be certain of his victory. Someone reported to him that the squadron's ammunition supplies were running low. At 7:35 A.M., not quite two hours after the opening of the battle, Dewey ordered a pause. As the smoke began to lift, he could begin to assess the results of the five passes his cruisers had made down the Spanish line. "It was clear to me we did not need a very large supply to finish our morning's task," he wrote. The squadron drifted just beyond range of the shore batteries and rested.

During the break, Dewey ordered a second breakfast for the crews and called the captains to the *Olympia* for another conference. Hatches were opened and the men below decks were allowed topside for air. Calkins remembered the breakfast: "There were sardines, corned beef, and hardtack on a corner of the wardroom table, still encumbered by the surgeons' ghastly gear, which was all unstained, however." Indeed, American casualties had been astonishingly light: none killed, only six wounded, all aboard the *Baltimore.*

Afterward, American veterans of the battle looked back in wonder at the outcome. It was as though they had fought under some protective charm. "Under the miraculous providence which ordered the events of that day those six American ships steamed back and forth unharmed for nearly three hours," an officer of the *Baltimore* wrote. But Providence had shown little mercy to the Spanish. Nearly 400 Spanish sailors were killed or wounded.

The *Reina Cristina* had been battered to death and the *Castilla*'s guns were almost silent. The other ships were trapped in the little harbor at the Cavite arsenal. Still, the Spanish had not given up. At 11:15, Dewey signaled for a renewal of the action. The squadron concentrated its full attention on the cruiser *Don Antonio de Ulloa.* The luckless *Ulloa* shortly rolled over and sank in the shallow water of Cavite inlet.

The U.S. gunboat *Petrel* steamed into Cavite harbor and fired several shots. One by one, the flags were hauled down on the surviving Spanish vessels. The *Petrel* sent crews aboard to take formal possession, and then set each ship afire to complete the destruction. At about 12:30 P.M., the gunboat signalled the *Olympia:* "The enemy has surrendered." In a morning's work, the Asiatic Squadron had wrecked 10 Spanish vessels and captured the Cavite naval yard.

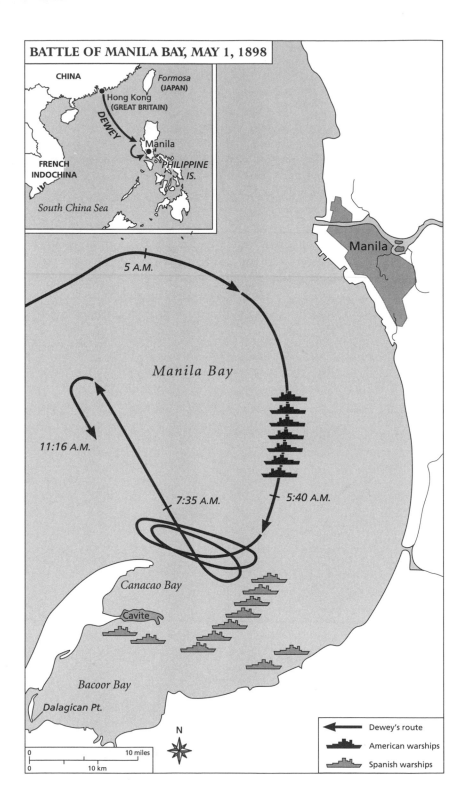

BATTLE OF MANILA BAY, MAY 1, 1898

CHINA

Formosa
(JAPAN)

Hong Kong
(GREAT BRITAIN)

DEWEY

Manila

PHILIPPINE
IS.

FRENCH
INDOCHINA

South China Sea

Manila

5 A.M.

Manila Bay

11:16 A.M.

7:35 A.M.

5:40 A.M.

Canacao Bay

Cavite

Bacoor Bay

Dalagican Pt.

N

0   10 miles
0   10 km

Dewey's route

American warships

Spanish warships

Dewey took the victorious squadron to an anchorage just off the Manila waterfront. When the city's Spanish commander refused him permission to use the cable to flash news of the victory home, Dewey ordered it dredged up from the harbor mud and severed. At least the Spanish agreed to cease firing from the shore. Blockaded, and with all communication with the outside world cut off, they had, to be sure, little choice. "The city was virtually surrendered," Dewey wrote later. "I had established a base seven thousand miles from home which I might occupy indefinitely."

Washington, meantime, anxiously awaited word from the Asiatic Squadron. A full week passed. There were ambiguous reports from Madrid. A rumor spread that Dewey's ships had been sunk. Finally, a New York *World* correspondent reached Hong Kong aboard the *McCulloch* and cabled the news. "I have just arrived here with my report of the great American triumph at Manila," he announced. "The entire Spanish fleet was destroyed. None of the American ships was injured." Five hours later, Dewey's official report reached the Navy Department. The obscure commodore became an instant national idol, as shown by this song verse.

> Dewey! Dewey! Dewey!
> Is the hero of the day!
> And the *Maine* has been remembered
> In the good old fashioned way.

President McKinley decided to seize and hold the Philippines, at least for the time being. He directed the War Department to assemble an expeditionary force in San Francisco. On May 13, Dewey cabled to report that he could take Manila at any time, but that a well-equipped force of 5,000 infantry would be required to control the archipelago. The first group of U.S. transports, carrying 2,400 troops, sailed for the Philippines on May 25.

The presence of a persistent Filipino named Emilio Aguinaldo complicated matters for Dewey. The 29-year-old son of a former clerk at the Cavite arsenal, Aguinaldo claimed leadership of the insurgent groups that were challenging Spanish colonial rule in the islands. The Spanish-American crisis seemed to offer Aguinaldo an opportunity he could not afford to miss.

Aguinaldo would claim later that American diplomatic officials in the Far East led him to believe the United States would support his

In 1898, 29-year-old Emilio Aguinaldo rose as the leader of the Philippine independence move-ment. *(Library of Congress, Prints & Photographs Division [LC-USZ62-93263])*

independence movement. At first, anyway, Dewey viewed him as a use-ful ally. An American warship carried Aguinaldo from Hong Kong to Manila during the third week in May. With the commodore's permis-sion, he set up insurgent headquarters at Cavite. Dewey also supplied the rebels with arms and ammunition for a landward advance on Manila.

Washington, however, shortly instructed Dewey to avoid any com-mitments to Aguinaldo and the insurgents. The islands, the McKinley administration suggested, were to be treated as spoils of war. To Wash-ington, they seemed ripe for the taking.

Dewey's sudden coolness did not deter Aguinaldo, whose forces went over to the offensive in late May. They soon controlled all of Cavite province and were closing in on Manila. Aguinaldo proclaimed Philippine independence on June 12, 1898. Eleven days later, he appointed himself head of the Philippine revolutionary government. By month's end, the first contingent of American infantry had reached Manila.

The seeds of a future imperial conflict had been sown. But at home, thousands of miles away, Americans were giddy with Dewey's success and flushed with war fever. Some, like their president, spun their globes in search of the exotic Philippines. Others, easily alarmed, pored over maps of Spain and the North Atlantic, trying to find the Spanish port city of Cádiz and the Cape Verde island group. The newspapers were reporting that a powerful Spanish squadron had put to sea and might be heading for the densely populated, rich, and practically undefended east coast of the United States.

4

THE WAR FROM
MAIN STREET

Neither the formal declaration of war on April 25 nor the rousing newspaper headlines had immediate impact on the lives of most Americans. There was no radio, let alone television; distant events did not affect people as directly as they would a century later. Commodore George Dewey's ships destroyed the Spanish fleet off Manila Bay on May 1, but the news of that event took a full week to reach America. Yet despite the remoteness and, as it would turn out, the brevity of this war of the summer of 1898, it nevertheless made an impression on American society.

There was little likelihood that the Spanish could carry the war to the continental United States. Still, naval experts agreed that the Spanish might make effective use of their warships by launching raids on Atlantic seaboard cities. "The patriotic citizens of the States may well come to rue the day that the meddling finger of Uncle Sam was thrust into the hornet's nest of Cuba," the British naval authority Frederick T. Jane wrote acidly. America's own preeminent sea power strategist, Alfred Thayer Mahan, believed that the Spanish fleet could serve a useful purpose merely by hovering just out of view over the horizon, where it would be "a perpetual menace" to the U.S. Navy, which could not guess when or where a blow might fall.

Speculation about Spanish intentions sent a current of fear running down the American East Coast. When the Spanish Atlantic squadron of Admiral Pascual Cervera y Topete sailed on April 29 from the Cape Verde Islands for an unknown destination, alarmist newspaper headlines

THE WAR FROM MAIN STREET

Crowds await the posting of war bulletins outside the New York Journal office, spring 1898. *(Library of Congress)*

fueled the scare. The Spanish force, four armored cruisers and three escorting destroyers, was out there in the gray wastes—somewhere. One eastern governor refused to let National Guard units leave his state, figuring he would need them to repel the Spanish. A congressman demanded a warship to protect the winter resort of Jekyll Island, Georgia. Seasonal residents of Newport, Rhode Island, were warned not to open their summer homes until the Spanish squadron had been dealt with. Boston businesses filled the vaults of banks in inland Worcester, Massachusetts, with cash, securities, and other valuables.

The Navy and War Departments were flooded with requests for troops and war vessels to defend the vulnerable cities. Senator William P. Frye, a Maine Republican who had lobbied energetically for intervention in Cuba, turned out to be one of the more persistent applicants once the shooting had started. "Senator Frye, who has been a blazing jingo, shouting for war, comes in with an appeal that a vessel be sent down to protect points along the coast," Navy Secretary John Long complained. Still, he sent a Civil War–era monitor-class ship to Portland, Maine's largest city. The announcement of its coming calmed fears there.

The Navy also formed a fast squadron to patrol the coast northward from the Delaware Capes to Bar Harbor, Maine.

In fact, Portland, Newport, Boston, and the other cities had next to nothing to fear from the Spanish. The excitement—panic, in some cases—would soon pass. The Spanish squadron sailed from its Cape Verde anchorage short of coal, with defective guns and ammunition, and with some ships in need of drydock repairs. Cervera, 59 years old, a sailor from the age of 12, had no confidence in his warships' ability to stand up to the American fleet. "The best thing would be to avoid war at any price," Cervera had said. As for raids on U.S. coastal cities, the Spanish admiral might have had difficulty even finding them. "We have no charts of the American seas," Cervera complained.

But Americans had little notion of Spanish naval deficiencies; a general attack of the jitters was perhaps to be expected in the circumstances. In any case, events of the 1890s had left many people with a chronic case of nervous anxiety. The comfortable classes were particularly susceptible: not just the rich in their summer homes, but the rapidly expanding middle class as well.

The United States in 1898 was just emerging from a long period of economic depression, political instability and social unrest. In the Populist uprising of 1892, farmers and laborers formed a powerful alliance to agitate for political and economic reform. The Populists called for government ownership of transportation, a graduated income tax, direct election of senators, and shorter working hours. Though the new party's presidential candidate polled less than 10 percent of the vote in 1892, the mainstream Democrats (and, later, the Progressive Republicans, too) incorporated many Populist proposals in their own political platforms.

Social protest often turned violent during these years. In Homestead, Pennsylvania, in 1892, striking workers fought street battles with the Carnegie Steel Company's private police and with state militia troops. The financial panic of 1893 threw thousands of Americans out of work. Hundreds of jobless men marched on Washington with "Coxey's Army," an organized movement seeking relief from unemployment. Banks collapsed. Businesses folded. There were a total of 1,400 strikes in 1894, some of them bloody. The great railroad strike of the summer of 1894 started among workers at the Pullman sleeping car factory in Chicago and soon spread to rail centers in all parts of the country. Federal troops were summoned to quell rioting in Chicago and

Oakland, California. The army eventually broke the strike and arrested its leader, the socialist Eugene V. Debs.

Social divisions were deepening among the 75 million Americans. With immigrants from southern and eastern Europe pouring into the United States by the tens of thousands, the foreign-born made up an increasing proportion of the total population—about 12 percent in 1898. Settling mostly in the large cities of the East and Midwest, the immigrants accelerated America's transition from a rural to an urban nation. Forty percent of Americans lived in towns with a population of 2,500 or larger, and the percentage was on the rise. Ninety percent of the country's nearly 9 million blacks lived in the rural South, but mass migrations to the northern industrial centers, where opportunities seemed greater, were already well under way.

Contradictions between American ideals and realities could be startling. At the end of March 1898, the U.S. Supreme Court, in a landmark decision, ruled that American citizenship is without regard to race or color. This meant that the American-born child of Chinese parents could not be deported under the infamous Chinese Exclusion Act of 1882. Less than two months later, however, white voters in Louisiana approved a new state constitution that effectively denied political rights to blacks by imposing strict property and literacy tests. Poverty, discrimination and neglect continued to ravage the American Indian population. There were scarcely 200,000 Native Americans in 1898, fewer than ever before in the history of European settlement.

Still, America was rich and growing richer, and conditions did seem to be improving for the majority of its citizens. Drought and crop failures in Russia sent wheat prices up in 1897 and 1898, easing American farmers' discontent. A skilled trade union worker might earn upwards of $1,000 a year, even if a common laborer's average annual wage was less than half that. Pay rates were even lower for women and children, and one child out of every five worked for wages. But at least jobs were plentiful again. The upturn in the business cycle after 1896 brought nearly full employment.

These were the great years of the Steam Age. More than 200,000 miles of railroad carried people and goods to every corner of the country. Coal-powered ships sped passengers across the Atlantic in a few days. Refrigerated steamers brought fresh winter fruit and vegetables from Florida and Bermuda to the frosty Northeast and Midwest. Signs of transition to new technologies were beginning to appear here and there.

Carts line bustling Orchard Street at the intersection of Rivington Street on the Lower East Side—a neighborhood composed mainly of immigrants—in New York City at the turn of the 20th century. *(Library of Congress, Prints & Photographs Division [LC-D4-71269])*

At the Biograph, an early moviemaker's view of American warships in action, 1898 *(Library of Congress)*

Electricity powered urban streetcar systems. Automobiles, first exhibited at the Chicago World's Fair of 1893, were seen on city streets occasionally. An Italian inventor named Marconi was experimenting with wireless telegraphy, trying to discover whether electromagnetic waves were practical for long-distance communication. Steam heat, electric light, running water, elevators, and telephones were no longer novelties.

For amusement, Americans turned to vaudeville, minstrel shows, musical comedies, and baseball (though the American League would not be established until 1901). "There'll Be a Hot Time in the Old Town Tonight!" became the hit song of 1898. Thousands of young volunteers were singing it in the army camps that were springing up everywhere. Jell-O, the "quick and easy dessert," first appeared on grocery shelves in the 1890s. In 1896, a North Carolina entrepreneur concocted a soft drink he called Pepsi-Cola, to compete with the popular Coca-Cola

Ragtime Goes to War

RAGTIME'S ORIGINS AS A MUSICAL FORM ARE OBSCURE, though it certainly derives from African-American folk music traditions of the plantation South. Ragtime gained its first wide audience at the World's Columbian Exposition in Chicago in 1893. By 1898 its "ragged" syncopated rhythms in vocal or instrumental versions were sweeping the country.

Bandleader Theodore Metz claimed his inspiration for the rag hit "There'll Be a Hot Time in the Old Town Tonight" came when he glanced out the window of his railroad car and glimpsed a group of children around a fire—they were either starting it or trying to douse it—near the tracks in Old Town, Louisiana. A band member remarked, "There'll be a hot time in Old Town tonight," and Metz jotted down the phrase. Eventually he used the phrase for the title of a march. Singer Joe Hayden added the lyrics, and a hit was born.

> There'll be girls for ev'rybody: In that good, good old town,
> For there's Miss Consola Davis and there's Miss Gondolia Brown
> And there's Miss Johanna Beasly she am dressed all in red,
> I just hugged her and kissed her and to me then she said:
> Please of please oh do not let me fall
> You're all mine and I love you best of all,
> And you must be my man, or I'll have no man at all,
> There'll be a hot time in the old town tonight.

With slightly altered lyrics, Metz's tune became a marching song for U.S. troops during the Spanish-American War. The "Rough Riders" volunteer cavalry adopted it as the regiment's official song.

introduced a decade earlier. Grape-Nuts and Shredded Wheat breakfast cereals were also newly available.

Thomas Edison's kinetoscope peep shows, early versions of the movies, were late-1890s fixtures in saloons, arcades, billiard rooms, and storefronts. The peeps were short subjects, moving pictures of jugglers and dancing girls—in one unusual version, 90 seconds of a man sneezing. By 1896, recordings of music could be purchased and played on a Victor Talking Machine Company phonograph. Victor's logo soon became famous the world over—a small black and white dog, Nipper, listening to "His Master's Voice." Later in 1898, Biograph motion picture cameras would record the victorious Admiral Dewey's triumphal homecoming from Manila Bay.

With the return of prosperity in the late 1890s came a steady increase in the cost of living—by as much as one-third, by some estimates, from

A drawing by Charles Dana Gibson depicts the ideals of style and beauty in 1898 New York. *(Library of Congress, Prints & Photographs Division [LC-USZ62-125425])*

1897 to 1900. The outbreak of war in the spring of 1898 helped fuel the rise. The cost of mules, still a main source of transportation, especially in country districts, nearly doubled, from $70–$90 to $130–$150 a head. The price of bunting—the essential red, white, and blue component of any patriotic celebration—increased by 300 percent.

Most Americans accepted conflict with Spain with lighthearted enthusiasm. "In April, everywhere, flags were flying," the Kansas journalist William Allen White wrote. "Trains carrying soldiers were hurrying to the Southland; and little children on fences greeted the soldiers with flapping scarves and handkerchiefs and flags." Flagmakers quickly sold out their stock. In New York, sales of Joseph Pulitzer's *World* soared, reaching 1.3 million copies a day by the end of April.

Celebrities offered their services to the nation—Buffalo Bill Cody, Frank James (brother of the notorious outlaw Jesse James, killed by a turncoat member of his own gang in 1882), the baseball star Cap Anson. Rudyard Kipling, the bard of the British Empire, urged Americans to "take up the white man's burden," that is to say, to follow the European inclination for imposing colonial rule over supposedly primitive African and Asian territories. Many Americans responded to Kipling's appeal, though few could foresee the long-term consequences of the emergence of the United States as a world power.

There were a few, a very few, dissenters. In Kansas City, a cobbler hung crape over his workshop door and put up this notice: "Closed in memory of a Christian nation that descends to the barbarity of war." Socialite Helen Gould was more typical in her enthusiasm, even if her means of expressing it were eccentric: she donated a yacht to the war effort, and $100,000 in cash to the U.S. Treasury. Another wealthy patriot, William Astor Chandler, raised and equipped a regiment of volunteers out of his own deep pockets. The navy supplied America with its first heroes of the Spanish war. Dewey of Manila became the toast of the nation. Restaurants served "ices à la Dewey," which were molded into the shape of warships. Commodore Winfield Scott Schley of the romantically named "Flying Squadron" became a national idol, too, as did Richmond Hobson, the gallant young officer who steered an ancient steamer straight into Spanish guns in a bold bid to block a Cuban harbor. The army fared less well. The press decided early on that readers craved news not of the "regulars" (and especially not of the four regular regiments of black troops, two of infantry and two of cavalry) but of the volunteers. Stephen Crane wrote:

In a burst of patriotism, *Leslie's Weekly* magazine turns its cover into a recruiting poster. *(National Archives)*

The public wants to learn of the gallantry of Reginald Marmaduke Montmorency Sturtevant, and for goodness sake how the poor old chappy endures that dreadful hard-tack and bacon. Whereas, the name of the regular soldier is probably Michael Nolan and his life-sized portrait was not in the papers in celebration of his enlistment.

Comparatively few of the nearly 200,000 volunteers managed to get overseas. Perhaps that was just as well, for many of the new soldiers were simple souls. A visiting civilian recalled approaching a camp guard of the 161st Indiana with this question: "Are you a sentinel, sir?" "No, I am a Swede," the soldier replied.

Boredom would shortly set in. People on Main Street began to lose interest in the boys in the dusty camps beyond the outskirts of town as stirring reports of land and sea battles in distant places began to fill the papers. The volunteers amused themselves with time-honored soldier pastimes: sports, gaming, liquor. Troops at Camp Alger, Virginia, dubbed the powerful local moonshine "two-step"—after drinking it, nobody could take more than two steps before falling down. Soon there were ailments more serious than a hangover. Typhoid fever and dysentery swept the stateside camps, especially in the warm, damp climates of Tennessee and Florida.

As the summer advanced, critical voices began to be heard. Health conditions in the army encampments were scandalous. "This park as a camping place is incurably infected," an inspector wrote of Chickamauga, near Chattanooga, Tennessee. "Every breeze carries a stench." Newspapers began demanding explanations. They also gleefully reported quarrels between the army and the navy and dug up instances of graft and profiteering in government contracts. Pulitzer, the war hawk of early 1898, began to campaign for peace. The war was costing his newspaper too much, his enemies whispered, especially in cable charges from the battlefronts.

War scarcely altered the routines of ordinary civilians. War news provided dinner table conversation; war matters were addressed from the pulpit on Sunday morning. The springtime panic over the Spanish cruisers in the Atlantic abated quickly. No Spanish shells exploded on American soil; the Spanish warships never approached the American coast.

The pessimistic Admiral Cervera's squadron wandered about the Caribbean during the first two weeks of May, venturing as far west as Curaçao off the coast of Venezuela before turning back toward Cuba. Commodore Schley's Flying Squadron hurried down from the Virginia Capes to search out the Spanish. Cervera called at the French island colony of Martinique for coal, found little, and had to leave at the order of the local port authorities, who were enforcing the neutrality laws. He decided to steer for Santiago de Cuba, a good, well-defended harbor on the southeast coast of the island. The Spanish cruisers safely cast anchor there at 8 A.M. on May 19.

The Spanish high command expected Cervera to refit in Santiago and move out to meet the Americans. But the ships' boilers needed cleaning. The engines needed overhauling. Coal supplies were nearly exhausted. Cervera's gloom deepened. "If we are blockaded before we can finish taking coal, which is scarce, we shall succumb with the city," he cabled Madrid. Schley's warships arrived to take up position off the harbor entrance, shutting Cervera in. Still, the Spanish admiral and his officers were feted in the town. The archbishop of Santiago toasted the squadron's anticipated attack on Washington, D.C. One of Cervera's captains recalled a profound feeling of sorrow as he listened to the archbishop. "We knew that our fate was already decided and that we were irredeemably lost," he wrote.

To the north, young Americans streamed into the volunteer camps. And Cervera's squadron continued to obsess the U.S. war planners. They decided that the expeditionary force now assembling at Tampa, Florida, would be landed near Santiago, to help the navy capture or destroy the Spanish warships. Americans could read all about the coming campaign in their newspapers. They could open the *World* and the *Journal* and the others to the inside pages, which carried ink-smudged maps of the Caribbean, and draw their fingers along the outline of Cuba's south coast until they found Santiago, haven for Cervera's fear-inspiring fleet and destination for the more than 15,000 men of the U.S. Army's V Corps.

5
MOBILIZATION

Large-scale maps of the Caribbean, Europe, and the Philippines on the walls of the White House war room showed war objectives and the disposition of forces in May 1898. Off Cuba, U.S. warships ran down blockade-runners and, from time to time, bombarded Spanish positions on shore. In the White House, clerks monitored 15 telephones and 25 telegraph instruments. Couriers rushed here and there with the latest bulletins. The commotion at the White House and the purposeful activity of the blockading fleet implied cool, capable, and firm direction of the war. Even the string band that entertained the blockade-weary officers of the USS *New York* at mealtimes fed the illusion: all was proceeding according to intelligent design.

In fact, the U.S. war machine coughed to a start, then lurched ahead in a series of unsteady jerks. The navy may have had a war plan; the army had none. The navy may have been prepared for war; the army lacked nearly everything—arms and ammunition, horses, mules and wagons, clothing and medical supplies. Phones trilled, telegraphs clacked, and aides stuck pins in the wall maps, but no one in the war room seemed to have much expertise in training and equipping an expeditionary force or transporting one overseas. U.S. troops had not even been formed for brigade drill in more than 30 years. Even regimental-strength field maneuvers were rare. (Regiments, ordinarily including up to 1,000 troops, were the army's basic unit of organization. Two or more regiments formed a brigade, and two or more brigades formed a division.)

More than 1 million young men had answered President William McKinley's April 23 call for 125,000 volunteers; they were eager to risk

A prospective volunteer studies an enlistment poster outside a New York City postal station, spring 1898. *(National Archives)*

wounds or fever on a private's wages of $13 a month, unchanged from the days of the Civil War. Potential recruits were given a not very rigorous medical examination: a jumping test for the heart, a coughing test to check for hernia, and an eyesight test. Enlistment quotas rapidly filled. Three-quarters of the applicants were turned down. The lucky ones—anyway, they thought themselves lucky—soon began to assemble in five large camps in Virginia, Georgia, Florida, Alabama, and California.

Prominent politicians obtained senior military appointments. William Jennings Bryan, the once and future Democratic presidential candidate, arranged to be made the colonel of a Nebraska volunteer regiment. Consul Fitzhugh Lee and Congressman Joseph Wheeler, both ex-Confederates, donned the formerly detested federal blue. Former Assistant Secretary of the Navy Theodore Roosevelt, now a volunteer army lieutenant colonel, set out from Washington in early May for the dusty training ground of the First U.S. Volunteer Cavalry—the Rough Riders—in San Antonio, Texas.

The Sixth Massachusetts, one of the few established National Guard regiments considered properly trained and equipped for war service, headed, via Baltimore, for the encampment in Tampa, Florida. Here was a regiment with a history. Angry mobs had stoned the Sixth Massachusetts when it passed through Baltimore on the way to Washington, D.C.,

Fighting for the Old Flag

THEY HAD BEEN AGGRESSIVE COMMANDERS OF Confederate cavalry in what they called the War Between the States: Joseph Wheeler in the West, where he gamely but futilely contested William T. Sherman's March to the Sea in 1864; Fitzhugh Lee in the East, where he fought in the Army of Northern Virginia under his larger-than-life uncle, Robert E. Lee.

President McKinley turned to both elderly Confederates in the spring of 1898, not only for their considerable military skills, but also as symbols of reconciliation between the North and the South 33 years after the Confederate surrender at Appomattox Court House.

Wheeler, born in Georgia, graduated from West Point in 1859, fought for the Confederacy for four years, and served as a congressman from Alabama from 1884 to 1900. Owing to his age (61 in 1898), he at first declined the appointment as major general of volunteers. Reasoning it would accelerate North-South healing, he reconsidered and landed in Cuba as commander of the Cavalry Division and second in command (to Gen. William Rufus Shafter) of the U.S. expeditionary force. He led frontline troops in battle at Las Guásimas and on San Juan Heights.

Lee, an 1856 West Point graduate, former governor of Virginia and U.S. consul general in Havana at the time of the sinking of the battleship *Maine*, also had been a spokesman for North-South reunion. He commanded the VII Corps in Florida, but the war ended before the corps could be made ready for overseas duty.

The contributions of Wheeler and Lee transcended their brief military service. In part because of their example, the U.S. Army after the Spanish-American War once again became a truly national institution.

in April 1861. In the spring of 1898, Maryland crowds pelted the Bay State troops with flowers.

The Rough Riders, authorized to accept 1,000 enlistees, were overwhelmed with applicants. "Without the slightest trouble, we could have raised a brigade or even a division," claimed Roosevelt, the regiment's second in command. A number of the volunteers were politically connected—Roosevelt, of course; the regimental commander, Col. Leonard Wood, President McKinley's personal physician; and Hamilton Fish, grandson of a secretary of state. Some were socially prominent—Harvard friends of Roosevelt's, other Ivy Leaguers, a member of the Tiffany jewelers' family.

The rank-and-file Rough Riders were a diverse crowd: cowboys and trappers, former college football stars, a steeplechase rider, a polo player, the one-time captain of crew at Columbia College, an ex-Texas Ranger, an ex-marshal of Dodge City, four former New York City policemen, and four ex-clergymen. Most of the men in the ranks were southwesterners from the Arizona, New Mexico, Oklahoma, and Indian Territories, colorful characters from both sides of the law. "Some of them went by their own name," Roosevelt wrote; "some had changed their names; and yet others possessed but half a name, colored by some adjective, like Cherokee Bill, Happy Jack of Arizona, Smoky Moore, and Rattlesnake Pete." The most foul-mouthed and blasphemous of the recruits answered to Prayerful James.

Wood's and Roosevelt's political wire-pulling gave the Rough Riders a running start over the other volunteer regiments. Uniforms, shelter tents, and horse gear were obtained, as well as the much-prized Krag-Jorgensen carbines, which fired smokeless powder. Wood, a regular army surgeon, worked the War Department supply bureaus; Roosevelt had a word with his friends in the railroad business to arrange express delivery of the goods. The Rough Riders drilled daily on the hot, dry plains around San Antonio.

Roosevelt soon declared himself satisfied with the regiment's appearance. "In their slouch hats, blue flannel shirts, brown trousers, leggings and boots, with handkerchiefs knotted loosely around their necks, they looked exactly as a body of cow-boy cavalry should look," he said.

Few other new regiments were yet in a condition to preen. Volunteers sweated in thick blue woolen uniforms; the army had no stores of tropical clothing to issue to them. They drilled with obsolete Springfield

Theodore Roosevelt (left) and Richard Harding Davis in camp near Tampa, Florida *(Library of Congress)*

rifles. The mess tins were Civil War relics, too. There were no bakers, so there was only hard bread. Spring rains deluged the Virginia, Georgia, and Florida camps. There were early reports of measles, typhoid, and other camp diseases. Medicines were in critically short supply. "Everything had to be extemporized," one volunteer officer remembered. A recruit in an Illinois cavalry regiment, perhaps recalling the flags and the cheering as his troop train rattled southward, wrote forlornly of the realities of soldier life:

> Pictures of flashing sabers and charging horses are very inspiring to look at, but an hour's saber drill with the thermometer at 105 degrees and riding horses bareback in a blinding dust three miles to water is a little more practical.

Regular army units and a few volunteer regiments converged on Tampa, the staging area for the invasion of Cuba. The Seventy-first New

A view of the U.S. Infantry camp in Tampa, where troops mobilized before being sent to Cuba. *(Library of Congress, Prints & Photographs Division [LC-USZ62-92728])*

York, another National Guard regiment, considered itself fortunate to receive orders to move to Florida while newly raised units remained in camps at home. The Seventy-first's experience suggests some of the confusion, disorder, and incompetence that came near to turning the U.S. mobilization into a farce.

The regiment shuffled aboard the coastal steamer *Seneca* in New York harbor before dawn on May 13. The troops found the ship overcrowded and shabby, the food—"sowbelly" served from a communal kettle—inedible. "As [each soldier] reached the galley door and was handed his cube of morbid pig, he would walk to the rail and toss it overboard," Pvt. Charles Post recalled. The ship lay at anchor off Hoboken, New Jersey, for two miserable days. Then came orders to disembark. Adm. Pascual Cervera's cruisers were at large, the men were told; to guarantee a safe transit, the Seventy-first would move by rail. Days behind schedule, the New Yorkers finally reached a temporary camp at Lakeland, Florida, 30 miles west of Tampa, toward the end of May.

While the troops assembled, the army and the navy argued about how—and how soon—the expeditionary force would be deployed. The force, designated V Corps, could not possibly move until the end of June, the army commander in chief, Gen. Nelson A. Miles, advised McKinley and the cabinet. By then the rains would have begun, and it would be high season in Cuba for yellow fever. Miles went on to recommend delaying the invasion until autumn. But the navy argued for immediate action, and McKinley sided with the admirals. Under pressure, the secretary of war, Russell A. Alger, promised on May 2 that the army would be ready to land 30,000 to 40,000 men in Cuba within a month.

Alger, a 62-year-old Civil War veteran and former governor of Michigan, would later bear much of the blame for the army's unpreparedness. In fairness, Alger inherited a hidebound, inefficient system when he took over the War Department in March 1897. Still, he showed little aptitude for the task of modernizing the army, even after it became clear that war with Spain was likely. He also tended to play politics with senior appointments. Alger had, for example, insisted that command of V Corps go to a fellow Michigan man, Brig. Gen. William Rufus Shafter.

Shafter, also 62, was an immensely fat, sometimes lethargic and often short-tempered Civil War volunteer who had stayed on after 1865 to make a career of the army. He established his headquarters in the Tampa Bay Hotel on April 29. There, collected in groups on the hotel's long porches during what Richard Harding Davis called "the rocking chair period" of the war, staff officers, correspondents, contractors, confidence men, foreign military attachés, political hangers-on, and officers' wives met to gossip about General Shafter and his senior aides and to weigh the prospects for an immediate offensive.

"It is a real oasis in a real desert," Davis wrote of the hotel. "A giant affair of ornamental brick and silver minarets in a city chiefly composed of derelict wooden houses drifting in an ocean of sand." After the tedium of life on the Cuba blockade aboard the *New York,* Davis enjoyed his sojourn in Tampa. He recalled:

> Each night people gathered in the big rotunda while a band from one
> of the regiments played inside, or else they danced in the big ball-room.
> One imaginative young officer compared it to the ball at Brussels on
> the night before Waterloo; another, less imaginative, with a long iced

drink at his elbow and a cigar between his teeth, gazed at the colored electric lights, the palm-trees, the whirling figures in the ball-room, and remarked sententiously: "Gentlemen, as General Sherman truly said, *War is Hell.*"

Fitzhugh Lee turned up, looking, said Davis, like "a genial Santa Claus, with a glad smile and glad greeting for everyone." There were, however, few occasions for good fellowship out in the camps. All was muddle there. "Tampa lay in the pine-covered sand-flats at the end of a one-track railroad, and everything connected with both military and railroad matters was in an almost inextricable tangle," recalled Roosevelt, who arrived from San Antonio with the Rough Riders in early June. He found nobody to guide the regiment to its campsite. There were no rations. Roosevelt and the other officers bought the men food out of their own pockets.

That irregular method of provisioning worked for the Rough Riders. America's pervasive racism caused it to fail for the men of the Tenth Cavalry, one of the segregated U.S. Army's black regiments—the famous

Journalist Richard Harding Davis reported on the war for the *New York Journal. (Library of Congress, Prints & Photographs Division [LC-USZ62-112723])*

MOBILIZATION

Theodore Roosevelt (center), hand on hip, with Rough Rider officers
(National Archives)

"buffalo soldiers," so designated by the Indian tribes that had faced them in battle on the western frontier. When Capt. John Bigelow, a white officer, went into a restaurant on Tampa's pier to make arrangements for the Tenth's troopers to be fed there, he was turned away. "I was told by the lady who kept it that to have colored men eat in her dining-room would ruin her business," Bigelow reported.

General Miles came down from Washington to prod the 300-pound Shafter into stepping up the pace. Miles saw at once that Shafter could do little to hurry the preparations. The War Department's supply and transport systems seemed to have broken down irreparably. "I found [Tampa] crowded with an indiscriminate accumulation of supplies and war material," Miles wrote. "The sidings from the Port of Tampa for perhaps fifty miles into the interior were blocked with cars." Railcars arrived without paperwork identifying their contents. "Officers are obliged to break open seals and hunt from car to car to ascertain whether they contain clothing, grain, balloon material, horse equipments, ammunition, siege guns, commissary stores, etc.," Miles went on. While troops around Tampa suffered for clothing, a 15-car train loaded with uniforms lay for weeks on a sidetrack 25 miles away.

Henry B. Plant, the tycoon who had built the Tampa Bay Hotel and owned the single-track rail line, seemed to view the war as an opportunity to show off the attractions of his resort. "Passenger trains were continually running between Tampa and the Port, carrying crowds of sightseers and tourists; and the regular freight, passenger and express business of the Plant system between Tampa and Key West went on without interruption," one of Shafter's aides, Lt. John Miley, complained.

All the regiments received weapons and live ammunition eventually, though most of the volunteers were issued old rifles that used black powder. (In battle, the regulars would shun the volunteers, knowing that each black-powder discharge would send up a billow of smoke, drawing an accurate enemy return fire.) The men drilled and practice-fired in the steamy heat. The Seventy-first New York moved from the Lakeland camp to Tampa. The troops understood the implications of the move. "Now that we knew we were destined for Cuba would be among the first in the actual fighting, after daily drill the men began to line up before the chaplain's, tent," Private Post wrote. On the evening of June 7, word finally reached the troops to prepare to board the transports that would deliver V Corps to Cuba.

Relentless navy pressure forced the decision to invade. After weeks of wandering, Admiral Cervera's squadron reached the harbor of Santiago on Cuba's south coast. American warships stood in close to keep Cervera confined there. Richmond Hobson and his small volunteer crew tried to sink a collier in the channel at the harbor's mouth on the night of June 3. The attempt failed, and the possibility remained that Cervera might succeed in achieving a breakout.

Washington's fear of the Spanish cruisers had not abated. Adm. William Sampson, the commander of the blockading squadron, played on that fear in a dispatch to the Navy Department. "If 10,000 men were here, city and fleet would be ours within forty-eight hours," he cabled. "Every consideration demands immediate army movement. If delayed, city will be defended more strongly by guns taken from the fleet." As a result, the War Department on June 7 ordered Shafter in Tampa to "sail at once" for Cuba.

V Corps broke camp that night. "We were ordered to prepare at once to leave," Trooper A. F. Cosby of the Rough Riders wrote home. "We rolled up a sleeping blanket, half of a shelter tent, and poncho with such clothes and comforts as we could, together; threw this over our shoulder, put on our cartridge belts with 125 rounds, took our canteen and eating things, then added a haversack with some rations issued to us; and with our carbines we were ready." There were too few ships, so the cavalry regiments were told at the last minute to leave all but the officers' horses behind; the soldiers would fight on foot. Cosby and the other Rough Riders took to the sandy road after dark, heading for rendezvous with the train that would carry them to the port of Tampa.

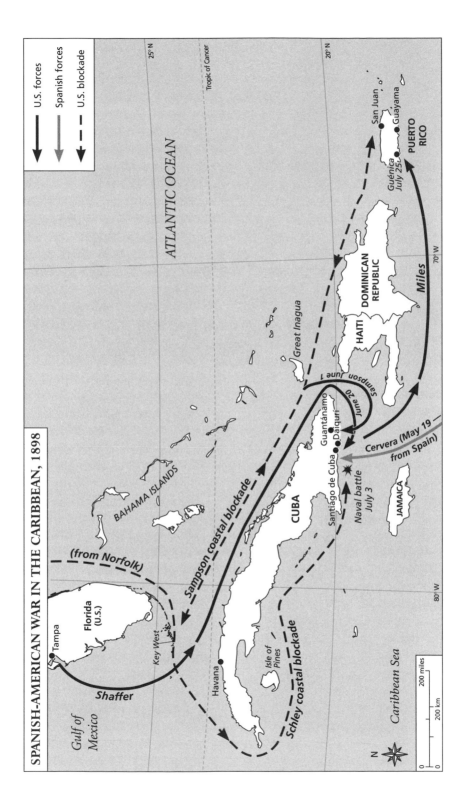

SPANISH-AMERICAN WAR IN THE CARIBBEAN, 1898

U.S. forces
Spanish forces
U.S. blockade

ATLANTIC OCEAN

25° N
Tropic of Cancer
20° N

San Juan
Guayama
PUERTO
RICO
Guénica
July 25
70° W
Miles

DOMINICAN
REPUBLIC
HAITI
Great Inagua
Sampson June 1

Guantánamo
Daiquiri
June 20
Cervera (May 19)
from Spain
Santiago de Cuba
Naval battle
July 3
JAMAICA
Sampson coastal blockade
CUBA
BAHAMA ISLANDS

(from Norfolk)
Florida
(U.S.)
Tampa
Key West
Schley coastal blockade
Havana
Isle of
Pines
Shaffer
Gulf of
Mexico
80° W
Caribbean Sea

N

0   200 miles
0   200 km

Chaos rules at pierside in Port Tampa, Florida, as troops embark for Cuba, June 1898. *(National Archives)*

Once again, conditions were chaotic. The train failed to turn up. "Worst confusion yet," Roosevelt wrote in his diary. "R.R. system is utterly mismanaged. No military at head. No allotment of transports. No plans." After a confused night, the regiment reached pierside in a coal train that Roosevelt had commandeered. There, the Rough Riders learned they had been assigned to the transport *Yucatan.* Roosevelt discovered by accident that two other units had been assigned to the ship, which was barely large enough for one full-strength regiment.

Roosevelt, who seems to have been at his swaggering, piratical best (or worst), resolved to attempt a second hijacking. "I ran down to my men and rushed them down to the dock and got on the *Yucatan,* holding the gangplank against the Second Infantry and the Seventy-first New York," he wrote. Roosevelt eventually relented slightly, allowing four companies of the Second Infantry, regulars, to embark with the Rough Riders.

The expeditionary force overwhelmed the port of Tampa's facilities, such as they were. Only two vessels could load at pierside at the same time. The rail line stopped short of the pier, so stevedores had to carry stores from the railhead across 50 feet of deep sand, up a steep ramp, and into the ships. Still, within 24 hours, an incredibly short time in the circumstances, 32 transports were packed with the largest military expedition ever to leave the United States: 16,000 officers and men, 89 correspondents, 30 civilian clerks, 2,500 horses and mules, 114 six-mule wagons, 81 escort wagons, seven ambulances, 16 field guns, four seven-inch howitzers, four five-inch siege guns, a dynamite gun, four Gatling guns, and eight mortars.

Word came on June 9 that Washington had postponed the convoy's sailing date, due to Cervera again, and his ramshackle fleet. Spanish warships—phantom vessels, it turned out—had been sighted in the San Nicolas Channel between Cuba and the Bahamas. The overcrowded troopships rocked at their moorings under a blistering Florida sun. The food was terrible, especially the article labeled "canned fresh beef." Roosevelt sympathized with the men's complaints. "At the best it was stringy and tasteless; at the worst it was nauseating," he reported. There were no vegetables and no ice.

The convoy finally sailed on June 14, bands playing, flags flying, soldiers cheering. The transports and their escorts steamed slowly south and east toward Santiago, nearly 1,000 miles distant. It was an agreeable

Troops of the Ninth U.S. Infantry board a Santiago-bound transport.
(National Archives)

voyage, "a succession of sparkling, sunlit days," wrote Richard Harding Davis, "undisturbed by Spanish cruisers or by shells from Spanish forts." Characteristically, Davis reached for a sporting image:

> Scattered over a distance of seven miles, the black passenger steamers and the mouse-colored war-ships steamed in three uneven columns and suggested a cluster of excursion steamers, and yachts and tugs as one sees them coming back from Sandy Hook after an international yacht race.

Even Davis admitted that yacht club amenities were altogether lacking below the decks of the troopships. The men continued to complain about the tasteless food and tepid water. "It smelled like a frog pond or a stable-yard," Davis said of the water, "and it tasted as it smelt." For some reason, Rough Rider Cosby had expected the fare to improve aboard

The Eastern Squadron

WHEN THE U.S. EMBASSY IN MADRID REPORTED IN mid-June that a Spanish battle fleet had sailed for the Philippines, the U.S. Navy responded with orders to assemble a powerful squadron to raid the virtually undefended Spanish Atlantic and Mediterranean coasts.

With its only seaworthy battleship, *Pelayo,* leading the way, the Spanish fleet under Adm. Manuel Cámara y Libermoore steamed slowly for the Philippines to confront Adm. George Dewey's Asiatic Squadron and relieve the beleaguered garrison of Luzon Island. The Americans moved to detach the powerful battleships *Iowa* and *Oregon* and the cruiser *Brooklyn* from the squadron blockading Cuba for raids and bombardments of Spanish ports. The United States leaked the plans, hoping they would encourage the Spanish to recall the Philippines fleet to protect the homeland.

The bluff, if that is what it was, served its purpose. Delayed at Suez by a British refusal to supply coal for his vessels, Cámara finally entered the Red Sea. On July 7, Spain's minister of marine ordered Cámara's fleet to turn back for home. The American warships never left the Caribbean.

ship. He was disappointed. "Coffee, hardtack, with canned beef, canned tomatoes and beans," he wrote home. "We get the coffee hot, but the other things are usually cold unless an enterprising fellow will make a mess of the whole thing which he calls a stew." Cosby worried that the poor diet would cause many men to lose weight and strength.

Still, these were, after all, minor flaws. The convoy proceeded toward Santiago free of military incident or the outbreak of serious illness. It was the beginning of a run of incredible American luck. "The foreign attachés," observed Davis, "regarded the fair weather that accompanied us, the brutal good health of the men, the small loss of horses and mules, and the entire freedom from interference on the part of the enemy with the same grudging envy that one watches a successful novice winning continuously at roulette." The transports steamed on with lights burning brightly at night, the regimental bands thumping out ragtime. Davis went on:

> There was nothing to prevent a Spanish torpedo-boat from running out and sinking four or five ships while they were drifting along, spread out over the sea at such distance that the vessels in the rear were lost to sight for fourteen hours at a time, and no one knew whether they had sunk or been blown up, or had grown disgusted and gone back home. As one of the generals on board said, "This is God Almighty's war, and we are only his agent."

Aboard the *Yucatan*, the Rough Riders caught sight of the Cuban coast on the morning of June 20. "High mountains rose almost from the water's edge, looking huge and barren across the sea," wrote Roosevelt. As the troops prepared to go ashore, the senior army and navy commanders continued to wrangle. Admiral Sampson, preoccupied with Cervera's squadron, wanted a frontal assault on the Santiago harbor defenses. General Shafter, cautious and deliberate, decided instead to put V Corps ashore on what appeared to be a deserted stretch of beach near Daiquirí, 15 miles east of the Santiago stronghold.

6
ASHORE IN CUBA

Richard Harding Davis saw irony in the army-navy dispute over where the Americans were to land. "It has often happened that an army has asked the navy to assist it in an assault upon a fortified port," he wrote. "But this is probably the only instance when a fleet has called upon an army to capture another fleet." Adm. William Sampson did not wish to risk his ships in the minefields of the inner harbor at Santiago. Gen. William Shafter did not wish to risk his men against the Spanish fortifications.

"We were a long way from the Civil War," one of Shafter's aides wrote, paraphrasing the general; "the country was no longer accustomed to hear of heavy losses in battle and would judge us accordingly; he intended to get his army into position around the city of Santiago and force a surrender."

Shafter landed on June 20 to meet the commander of the Cuban insurgents in the district, Gen. Calixto García, and to scout potential landing places. U.S. Marines were already ashore at Guantánamo, 40 miles east of Santiago. After a brief skirmish with the Spanish, they established a coaling station there for the blockading fleet. But Shafter decided against Guantánamo. It was too far from his objective, and the roads were poor. On García's recommendation he chose Daiquirí, 25 miles closer to Santiago. The limestone bluffs dominating the Daiquirí beach looked formidable, but the Cubans assured Shafter that they were lightly defended. Besides, 1,500 *insurrectos* covered the invasion force. Without them, as the Spanish general Valeriano Weyler remarked afterward, "the Americans would not have been able to effect their landing." Shafter ordered that the landings begin at Daiquirí on the morning of June 22.

ASHORE IN CUBA

Six American warships opened the affair with a bombardment of suspected Spanish positions on the bluffs. After 20 minutes or so, a troop of Cuban insurgent cavalry cantered onto the beach, signaling that the enemy had gone. "Soon the sea was dotted with rows of white boats filled with men bound about with white blanket-rolls and with muskets at all angles, and as they rose and fell on the water and the newspaper yachts and transports crept closer and closer, the scene was strangely suggestive of a boat race, and one almost waited for the starting gun," wrote Davis. From the headquarters transport, he watched the longboats and launches steer for the beach under cover of smoke from the naval guns.

Davis had counted on going ashore with the first wave, and he waited with mounting anger for Shafter to allow the correspondents to land. The general refused to let Davis and the others accompany the assault troops. Davis protested; he was a "descriptive writer," he told Shafter, not a correspondent. Shafter, experiencing understandable anxiety about the military operation, may have been suffering from the heat as well. For whatever reason, the overweight general lost his temper. "I do not care a

This drawing shows the beginning of debarkation of troops at the Daiquirí beach in Cuba. *(Library of Congress, Prints & Photographs Division [LC-USZ62-91363])*

damn what you are," he barked at Davis. "I'll treat you all alike." Davis and the other correspondents were furious. "From the moment of issuing that order pencils began to be sharpened for General Shafter," one of the reporters wrote later. The journalists eventually would have their revenge, subjecting Shafter's management of the campaign to intense, sometimes unfair criticism.

The boats landed through a heavy swell. The horses and mules were turned out from the ships and pointed in the direction of the beach. Some animals, confused, headed out to sea and disappeared. Others swam in circles until they exhausted themselves and drowned. Finally someone suggested tethering large groups of animals together and towing them ashore. The men had somewhat better success, though two troopers of the Tenth Cavalry drowned when their boat overturned in the surf.

The first troops to land found Daiquirí abandoned. There was little to explore: the machine shops of the Spanish-American Iron Company, a few zinc shacks, and several rows of palm-thatched huts. The Spanish had set fire to the shops and a long row of railcars before retreating beyond the bluffs toward Santiago, extending the Americans'

The Spanish burned these locomotives at Daiquirí before retreating as the U.S. troops landed. *(National Archives)*

run of luck. "Five hundred resolute men could have prevented the disembarkation at very little cost to themselves," said Roosevelt, whose Rough Riders were in the first wave of the landing. But the Spanish did not fire a shot. More than 6,000 men were ashore by the evening of June 22.

The Americans now met their first Cuban insurgents. Contacts, then and later, were not cordial. The Americans consistently understated or even refused to acknowledge the Cubans' role, rarely mentioning the insurgents except to complain about their shortcomings. The Cubans were short of everything. The Americans appeared to possess abundant supplies of clothing and food. The Cubans, in their rags and bare feet, expected help from their new allies; the Americans viewed the insurgents as little better than beggars. Reporter John Askins wrote:

> Whenever one lighted a fire a Cuban presented himself, at the sign of the smoke, quietly and inexplicably like a genie, and asked for food. The Cuban insurgent regarded every American as a kind of charitable institution, and expected him to disgorge on every occasion. The Cuban was continually pointing to the American's shirt, coat or trousers, and then pointing to himself, meaning that he desired a transfer of property.

Land crabs, stinging insects, and flying pests were far more trouble than the Spanish that first night. The land crabs, similar to the marine variety, were large, some of them as big as a mess tin, with two long pincers. At night they emerged from their hiding places by the hundreds, making an unnerving rustling sound as they scuttled through the underbrush. Jumpy pickets fired toward the disturbances. Some Sixth Infantry soldiers were involved in a sharp skirmish with a large party of land crabs. "The fight lasted all night long and they almost drove us from our position," one rifleman remembered. Rain fell. There were sand flies, gnats, spiders, scorpions, and the Cuban jigger, whose bite, the troops had been warned, could be fatal.

The route to Santiago ran westward to the beachfront town of Siboney, then turned inland through a gap in the coastal range of hills. At daybreak on June 23, a column of two infantry regiments moved up to Siboney. The Americans found the place deserted. By noon troops were being landed there. The operation continued deep into the night.

Davis, ashore finally, described the scene, which was lit by the glare of the ships' searchlights:

> An army was being landed on the enemy's coast at the dead of night, but with somewhat more of cheers and shrieks and laughter that rise from the bathers in the surf at Coney Island on a hot Sunday. The men were dancing naked around the campfires on the beach, or shouting with delight as they plunged into the first bath that had offered in seven days, and those in the launches as they were pitched headfirst at the soil of Cuba, signalized their arrival by howls of triumph.

Davis trudged inland, accompanying a column of dismounted cavalry that included the Rough Riders. The men pushed out after dark to a point three miles beyond Siboney, near a place where two trails met called Las Guásimas. The Spanish rear guard had entrenched there. Joe Wheeler, commanding the cavalry division, ordered an assault for the morning of June 24.

Wheeler sent a column of regulars out on the main road at sunrise. The Rough Riders, with Davis and other correspondents attached, advanced on a parallel track through dense woods. "They wound along this narrow, winding path, babbling joyously, arguing, recounting, laughing; making more noise than a train going through a tunnel," correspondent Stephen Crane wrote. After a while, Col. Leonard Wood, the regimental commander, called a halt. A little later, he ordered the Rough Riders to fan out on either side of the trail. Up ahead, firing broke out.

"The air seemed full of the rustling sound of the Mauser bullets," Lt. Col. Theodore Roosevelt recalled. The Rough Riders could see nothing through the forest. They advanced slowly, the detachments on the flanks soon disappearing from sight. "It was like forcing the walls of a maze," Davis wrote. The firing soon became general. Trooper A. F. Cosby sent his mother this description of the first land battle of the war:

> We went blindly down a hill, I heard the scream or whine of bullets, saw dust fly & heard little explosions. I did not see the enemy or smoke but we fired a couple of rounds in their direction to try our guns. We did this for 3 hours tramping up and down as fast as we could.

Casualties began to mount. The correspondent Edward Marshall saw many men shot. "Everyone went down in a lump without cries, without

Gen. Joseph Wheeler and staff: Wheeler led the cavalry division in the advance on Santiago in late June 1898. *(U.S. Army Military History Institute)*

jumping in the air, without throwing up hands. They just went down like clods in the grass," he wrote. Soon Marshall himself fell, shot in the spine. Stephen Crane found him lying still in the hot grass. He recorded the encounter.

"Hello, Crane!"

"Hello, Marshall! In hard luck, old man?"

"Yes, I'm done for."

"Nonsense! You're all right, old boy. What can I do for you?"

"Well, you might file my despatches. I don't mean file 'em ahead of your own, old man—but just file 'em if you find it handy."

Crane and another man carried Marshall back to the aid station. (He survived.) On the main road, the regulars were advancing into a sharp and well-aimed fire. Wheeler sent back to Siboney for infantry reinforcements. The troopers crept on slowly toward the Spanish lines. Just as the first men of the infantry column appeared, the Spanish gave way.

Blurred figures could be seen retreating toward Santiago. Forgetting himself in the excitement, Wheeler, a former Confederate general, jumped up and down and called out: "We've got the damn Yankees on the run!"

The skirmish cost the Americans 16 killed and 52 wounded; Spanish casualties were 10 dead, 25 hurt. The Las Guásimas fight had one far-reaching consequence: the correspondents, especially Davis, made heroes out of the Rough Riders, especially the Rough Riders' ambitious lieutenant colonel, Theodore Roosevelt. The encounter had the military effect of clearing the road to Santiago as far as the San Juan Heights just east of the city. From high ground, Wheeler could see Santiago, some seven miles distant, and the Spanish in prepared positions on those protective hills.

General Shafter halted the offensive for several days to stockpile food, ammunition, and other supplies. Transport remained a problem. It was taking longer than Shafter had anticipated to unload the ships. The map designated the main Santiago route a "wagon road," an exaggeration, it turned out. Even after the engineers improved it, the road remained so narrow in places that only one wagon could pass at a time. Rainstorms converted the trail, which ran between earthen banks three or four feet high, into a gutter of flowing mud.

Tents were inadequate protection against the fierce tropical downpours. Tobacco rations failed to get through; deprived of this stimulant, the men "suffered just as greatly as a dipsomaniac who is cut off from alcohol," Davis thought. "We did not get quite the proper amount of food," Roosevelt complained, "and what we did get, like most of the clothing issued us, was fitter for the Klondyke than for Cuba." The climate was beginning to take a toll. Regimental sick lists lengthened: there were cases of tropical fevers, dysentery, heat exhaustion.

While Shafter struggled with the supply problem, the Spanish improved their defensive works. The main road and a parallel trail led through thick jungle to the foot of the San Juan Heights. From the high ground to the east, the Americans could observe the Spanish preparations. Davis wrote:

> We could see straw sombreros rising and bobbing up and down, and under the shade of the blockhouse, blue-coated Spaniards strolling leisurely about or riding forth on little white ponies. Rifle pits were growing in length and number, and the enemy was entrenching himself

at San Juan and at the little village of El Caney to the right, where he was marching through the streets.

In blockaded Santiago, where the Spanish commander, Gen. Arsenio Linares, had 13,000 troops to feed, hunger had become endemic among the civilian population. There were reports, too, of scattered outbreaks of fever. Still, Linares managed to prepare a formidable defensive line, which curved north to south to cover the eastern approaches to the city: 4,000 yards of trenches protected by barbed wire, with blockhouses at intervals and, at the hamlet of El Caney, a stone fort.

Buffalo Soldiers

TWO REGULAR REGIMENTS OF AFRICAN-AMERICAN troops, the Ninth and Tenth U.S. Cavalry—the famous "buffalo soldiers" of the frontier West—saw extensive fighting in Cuba during the Spanish-American War. (Their nickname supposedly originated with Indians who saw the African Americans' hair as resembling buffalo fur.) Both were involved in the assaults up the San Juan Heights for which Theodore Roosevelt and his Rough Riders later received most of the acclaim.

Some 9,000 African Americans joined the volunteer army in 1898. Alabama, Ohio, and Massachusetts formed black units during the first call for volunteers. President McKinley, mindful that 200,000 blacks had served the Union during the Civil War, accepted in the second call black units from four additional states. The army's only black regular officer, 1889 West Point graduate Charles Young, accepted a posting as commanding officer of a battalion of Ohio volunteers.

Most state National Guard regiments refused, however, to accept black enlistees, or at least gave preference for available places to white volunteers. African-American organizations campaigned for a larger role, on the theory that military service in wartime would accelerate social and economic gains afterward. Accounts of black bravery in Cuba were widely published in American newspapers. One headline read: THE NEGRO SOLDIER HAS WON UNBOUNDED RESPECT IN THE WAR WITH SPAIN. But apart from the regulars, only one other black unit—a company of the Sixth Massachusetts infantry, saw combat against the Spanish.

From a distance, Davis thought, the San Juan hills "looked so quiet and sunny and well-kept that they reminded one of a New England orchard." When the time came, the heights would prove to be anything but pastoral. The Spanish trained their guns on the openings where the only two trails available to the Americans emerged from the jungle onto a grassy open plain.

General Shafter, suffering intensely from the heat and from an untimely flare-up of gout, ordered a frontal attack for the morning of July 1. The direct approach, he judged, would be less costly in the long run. "If we had attempted to flank them out," he explained later, "my men would have been sick before it could have been accomplished." Shafter assigned Gen. Henry Lawton's division, 5,400 infantry, to assault El Caney. To the south, the dismounted cavalry and Jacob Kent's infantry division, 8,000 men altogether, were to cross the San Juan River and charge the rifle pits and entrenchments on the San Juan Heights.

The troops moved up to their start lines during the night of June 30, slogging in a downpour through mud three inches deep. Later, the skies cleared. "Three miles away, across the basin of mist, we could see the street lamps of Santiago shining over the San Juan Hills," Davis wrote. As the sun rose, the enemy trench lines came into clear view. "To the left of the first hill, holding a horse, stood one lone Spanish sentinel," recalled Lt. John J. Pershing of the Tenth Cavalry. The Americans opened fire on El Caney at 6:30 A.M. with four light guns. Lawton's infantry set out through tall grass a few minutes later.

"There was little target visible," Arthur Lee, the British military attaché, reported, "but the Spanish sharpshooters concealed in the trees, cottages and block-houses were replying with deadly effect. They knew every range perfectly and picked off our men with distressing accuracy if they showed so much as a head." There were barely 500 Spanish defenders, but they were well-placed and the Americans seemed confused. Wandering around, Arthur Lee encountered a detachment of 100 men in the shelter of a sunken road. He thought they were reserves; in fact, they were the dead and wounded. Long afterward, Lee remembered the eerie creaking of the land crabs off in the bushes, awaiting opportunity to feed off the corpses.

Too ill to come to the front, Shafter tried to direct the battle from his headquarters tent. He intended at first to launch the assault on the San Juan Heights after El Caney had been captured. With Lawton bogged down there, he ordered the San Juan attack to go ahead. The assault formations, Kent's infantry and Wheeler's dismounted cavalry, advanced down the jungle trails. The Spanish kept up an accurate fire, much of it aimed at an observation balloon the Americans had obligingly tethered over the cavalry lines. Davis wrote:

> A Spaniard might question if he could hit a man, or a number of men, hidden in the bushes, but had no doubt at all as to his ability to hit a mammoth glistening ball only six hundred yards distant, and so all the trenches fired at it at once, and the men of the First and Tenth (cavalry), packed together directly behind it, received the full force of the bullets. The men lying directly below it received the shrapnel which was timed to hit it.

The Seventy-first New York moved up along the narrow track. The Spanish fired high at the beginning, then gradually corrected their aim. "The first high bullets had been a thrill," Pvt. Charles Post wrote. "Now the bullets were proof that someone was trying to kill us, each one of us individually, and in a highly impersonal way." As the head of the column spilled out onto the open plain, the enemy loosed a hurricane of fire. Within minutes, reported Post, 400 men had been killed or wounded. Efforts to return fire actually made matters worse. Even a single shot from the Seventy-first's black-powder Springfield rifles triggered a Spanish volley into the telltale smoke cloud.

The wounded came in a steady stream to the aid station on the bank of the San Juan River. The artist Frederic Remington remembered watching a surgeon explore a chest wound, then turn away, shaking his head and motioning for the next case. "He held a wounded foot up to him, dumbly imploring aid, as a dog might," Remington wrote. "It made my nerves jump, looking at that grewsome hospital, sand-covered, with bleeding men." Davis later accused the Spanish snipers of deliberately shooting into the hospital and at the stretcher-bearers bringing in the wounded.

Spanish fire finally brought down the balloon. The American regiments forded the river and formed in battle order at the base of two hills. The cavalry sought cover opposite the rise on the right, dubbed Kettle Hill for the huge iron pot, part of a sugar refining works, on the summit. The infantry deployed to the left, opposite San Juan Hill. Roosevelt, now commanding the Rough Riders (Leonard Wood had

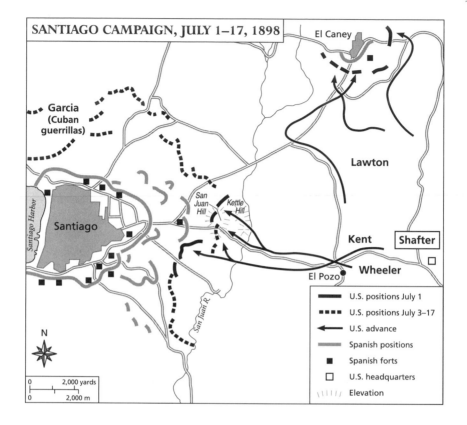

SANTIAGO CAMPAIGN, JULY 1–17, 1898

El Caney

Garcia
(Cuban
guerrillas)

Lawton

Santiago Harbor

Santiago

San
Juan
Hill

Kettle
Hill

Kent

Shafter

El Pozo

Wheeler

San Juan R.

N

	U.S. positions July 1
	U.S. positions July 3–17
	U.S. advance
	Spanish positions
■	Spanish forts
□	U.S. headquarters
||||	Elevation

0   2,000 yards

0   2,000 m

moved up to a brigade command), studied several large ranch buildings atop Kettle Hill.

The cavalry division lay in the heat under a steady fire, awaiting the
order to advance. The troopers' positions were untenable and they could
not retreat; the tracks for miles to the rear were jammed with troops and
transports. The Spanish musketry was too hot to endure much longer.
The ailing Shafter seemed unable to reach a decision. Lieutenant John
Miley, the aide who served as Shafter's representative at the front, finally
took the initiative. "The heights must be taken at all hazards," Miley told
the cavalry commanders.

When the order came, several cavalry regiments surged up Kettle
Hill in the face of a steady enemy fire. In the aftermath, all the acclaim
went to the Rough Riders. Legend and simplification obscured the
actual event. The Rough Riders charged Kettle Hill, not San Juan Hill.

Only the officers were mounted. The troopers fought on foot, as they did throughout the Santiago campaign. And the Rough Riders had lots of company on the way up the slope. Even Roosevelt, never bashful about publicizing his exploits, reported the assault as a combined effort of the full cavalry division. "The whole line, tired of waiting, and eager to close with the enemy, was straining to go forward; and it seems that different parts slipped the leash at almost the same moment," Roosevelt wrote. In Davis's words:

> There were a few men in advance, bunched together, and creeping up a steep, sunny hill, the tops of which roared and flashed with flame. The men held their guns pressed across their breasts and stepped heavily as they climbed. Behind these first few, spread out like a fan, were single lines of men, slipping and scrambling in the smooth grass, moving forward with difficulty, as though they were wading waist high through water, moving slowly, carefully, with strenuous effort. It was much more wonderful than any swinging charge could have been.

Some of the men went forward on hands and knees, the Rough Rider Frank Knox recalled, and crawled on their stomachs at times. To the left, the black regulars of the Ninth and Tenth Cavalry kept pace with the Rough Riders. The advance carried to the crest, where a large body of troopers took shelter behind the iron kettle. From the summit, the cavalry could see Jacob Kent's infantry charging up neighboring San Juan Hill. Roosevelt ordered the firing of volleys across the valley into the secondary Spanish positions, in support of the infantry assault.

A detachment of rapid-fire Gatling guns accompanied Kent's leading regiments, the Sixth and Sixteenth Infantry, spraying the Spanish positions with deadly effect and sending some of the defenders at a trot for the rear. "It was terrible when your guns opened," a captured Spanish officer told one of the machine gunners afterward. "They went b-r-r-r, like a lawn mower cutting the grass over our trenches. We could not stick a finger up without getting it cut off." The Americans came boiling up to the crest at a yell, forcing the remaining defenders to run, give up, or be shot.

With Kent's success on San Juan Hill, the Rough Riders and parts of several other regiments pushed across the valley to the second range of hills, Roosevelt in the lead. "When we reached these crests, we found

Theodore Roosevelt (center, with glasses) and his Rough Riders at the top of Kettle Hill. *(National Archives/DOD, War & Conflict #0299)*

ourselves overlooking Santiago," Roosevelt wrote. Here the trenches were deserted, except for a few Spanish dead. By 4:30 P.M., the firing had all but died out. To the north, Lawton's troops had finally subdued the Spanish at El Caney.

Roosevelt was not quite finished, however. Catching sight of two black cavalrymen heading down the hill, he sprang into action again. Assuming that the two were shirking, Roosevelt drew his revolver and threatened to shoot them. In fact, the regulars, black and white, had fought bravely. The troopers, it turned out, had been ordered to the rear for entrenching tools. When an officer explained the errand to Roosevelt, he agreed to spare their lives.

The July 1 fighting cost the Americans 205 dead, 1,180 wounded. Spanish casualties were 215 dead, 376 wounded. The numbers overwhelmed the U.S. medical services. Hundreds of wounded men lay exposed on the ground, broiling in the summer sun. "No organized or systematic provision had been made for feeding them or giving them drink, and many a poor fellow had not tasted food or water for twelve hours," the Red Cross official George Kennan reported.

Up in the hills, the exhausted survivors congratulated themselves. Stephen Crane wrote:

The army was dusty, dishevelled, its hair matted to its forehead with sweat, its shirt glued to its back with the same, and indescribably dirty, thirsty, hungry, and a-weary from its bundles and its marches and its fights. It sat down on the conquered crest and felt satisfied.

The Americans dug in. Rumors of a possible withdrawal began to circulate. Shafter evidently worried that the U.S. lines were overextended. Roosevelt sought reassurance from Joe Wheeler. "He had been through too much heavy fighting in the Civil War to regard the present fight as very serious, and he told us not to be under any apprehension, for he had sent word that there was no need whatever of retiring," Roosevelt reported. The night turned cool. A few of the Rough Riders huddled in blankets taken from the enemy. Firing broke out around 3 A.M., then again at dawn. But the Spanish did not venture an attack.

The second-guessing began immediately. "Our General is poor," Roosevelt wrote to his politically influential friend Henry Cabot Lodge two days after the battle. "He is too unwieldy to get to the front." Some volunteer officers and journalists accused Shafter of being ignorant of the battlefield, of ignoring sound advice from his subordinates, and of failing to supervise the battle. Doubtless remembering Shafter's impolitic outburst aboard the headquarters ship, Davis was withering:

General Shafter saw the field of battle only once before the fight took place. That was on June 29th, when he rode out to El Poso hill and surveyed the plain below. He was about the last officer in his army corps to climb that hill and make this survey, and he did not again go even that far to the front until the night after the battle. His trip to El Poso was apparently too much for his strength, and the heat during the ride prostrated him so greatly that he was forced to take to his cot, where he spent the greater part of his stay in Cuba.

From Davis's account, one might have thought the Americans had suffered a serious reverse. In fact, Shafter achieved substantial results. Dreading a yellow fever epidemic, he had forced the pace as far as conditions allowed. "I determined to rush it," Shafter wrote afterward, "and I did rush it." Only nine days after the initial landings, the Americans, with help from their Cuban allies, had overrun the main Spanish defenses and clapped a siege on their main objective, Santiago. Shafter sent his first surrender demand to the Spanish commander early on July 3. Later that morning, Admiral Cervera's warships steamed out of Santiago harbor in an effort to slip past the American blockading squadron.

7

SEA FIGHT
OFF SANTIAGO

The gunfire had hardly died out over the San Juan hills when the senior American commanders resumed their argument. Adm. William Sampson continued to call for a frontal assault on Santiago's fortifications, even though the land forces had almost completely sealed off the city by the morning of July 2. Gen. William Shafter, in turn, wanted the navy to force an entrance into the harbor and shoot up Adm. Pascual Cervera's ships at their moorings. "I am at a loss to see why the navy cannot work under a destructive fire as well as the army," he wrote Sampson.

Capt. Alfred Thayer Mahan, the theorist of sea power, supplied the answer. Ships, he argued, were more important than men. "If we lost ten thousand men, the country could replace them; if we lost a battleship, it could not be replaced," Mahan explained. "The issue of the war depended upon naval force. A million of the best soldiers would have been powerless in the face of hostile control of the sea."

So the soldiers dug in on the heights around Santiago while the sailors maintained their watch just offshore, illuminating the narrow harbor entrance with searchlights in case Cervera should try a breakout at night. The navy went about its work in relative comfort and with small likelihood of serious interference from the Spanish coastal guns; one of the cannons in Morro Castle dated from 1668, the Americans learned later, and five others had been cast in 1724. The infantry, of course, endured Spanish sharpshooters, occasional outbreaks of artillery, heat, dampness and discomfort, and the prospect of fever.

"If any one has discovered a more uncomfortable place to spend a hot day than in a four-foot trench, I have yet to hear of it," the Rough Rider Frank Knox wrote home. "One had to sit all cramped up with no opportunity to move; just sit there and fry and boil and sweat under the blistering sun and drink muddy water and chew an occasional hardtack."

After the battle at San Juan Heights, Shafter asked Gen. Joe Wheeler to scout the Spanish inner defenses and report whether they could be taken by assault. Using a powerful telescope and following the curve of

The Voyage of the Oregon

ANTICIPATING WAR, THE NAVY DEPARTMENT IN EARLY March 1898 ordered the battleship *Oregon* to steam without loss of a moment from the West Coast to the Atlantic. In the absence of a canal connecting the oceans where the North and South American continents join, the warship faced a voyage of nearly 14,000 miles.

In the 1880s, the French engineer Ferdinand de Lesseps, the builder of the Suez Canal linking the Mediterranean and the Red Sea, failed in his effort to cut a sea-level canal across the Isthmus of Panama. Some 20,000 laborers died in the attempt, victims of overwork and tropical diseases. *Oregon*'s long dash around Cape Horn would rekindle enthusiasm for a U.S.-built and -controlled interocean waterway.

The battleship left Bremerton, Washington, on March 7, 1898, for San Francisco, where it took on coal and ammunition. Then it sailed for Callao, Peru, its crew pushing the pace, straining to maintain an average speed of 11 knots an hour. "Life between decks became almost intolerable," one of its officers wrote, "for to the tropical heat was added that generated by the ship's boilers, kept at a full head of steam." Temperatures climbed to 115 degrees in the compartments directly above the boilers.

Oregon cleared the Straits of Magellan and turned northward during the third week in April. After calls for coal in Brazilian ports, the warship touched at Bridgetown, Barbados, before reaching Key West, Florida, on May 27 after a voyage of 66 days and 13,792 miles.

In July, the *Oregon* helped destroy the Spanish cruisers off Santiago, Cuba. But historians agree that the significance of its epic voyage lay in strengthening the resolve of American political, diplomatic, and military leaders to build a path between the oceans at any cost.

fortifications around Santiago, Wheeler carried out a thorough investigation. He thought the job might be done, but at a high cost: 3,000 U.S. casualties, he estimated, more than double the number of men killed and wounded in the San Juan hills. Shafter decided to be patient. Possibly the Spanish could be persuaded to surrender.

As it happened, the Spanish land and naval commanders were enmeshed in disagreements of their own. Ramón Blanco, the captain general in Havana, challenged Admiral Cervera to run the American blockade. Cervera responded that the attempt would end in his warships' certain destruction. Besides, he noted, some of his crews were ashore as infantry; the quick-firing naval guns could also assist in the defense of Santiago. Blanco persisted, arguing that losing ships in battle would be preferable to scuttling them in port. "If we should lose the squadron without fighting, the moral effect would be terrible, both in Spain and abroad," Blanco wrote Gen. Arsenio Linares, the army commander in Santiago.

Cervera rated his chances of successfully engaging the Americans as nil. His ships were in poor mechanical condition. His crews were scattered. His ammunition was defective. Leaving these issues aside, the Spanish were seriously outgunned: the American heavy ships carried 14 12- or 13-inch guns against only six 11-inch guns in the Spanish vessels; there were 30 American eight-inch guns against none of that caliber in the Spanish squadron. Blanco was proposing to send the navy on a death errand. Cervera wrote Linares:

> Today I consider the squadron lost as much as ever, and the dilemma is whether to lose it by destroying it, if Santiago is not able to resist, or whether to lose it by sacrificing to vanity the majority of its crews and depriving Santiago of their cooperation, thereby precipitating its fall. I state most emphatically that I shall *never* be the one to decree the horrible and useless hecatomb which will be the only possible result of the sortie from here by main force, for I should consider myself responsible before God and history for the lives sacrificed on the altar of vanity, and not in the true defense of the country.

Seven American warships, four battleships, a cruiser, and two small, swift escort vessels were on station three miles off Santiago the morning of Sunday, July 3. The *New York*, the flagship, was steaming eastward toward Daiquirí, carrying Admiral Sampson to a meeting with Shafter.

Sampson decided to keep the appointment even though his lookouts had seen columns of smoke rising above Santiago harbor the day before, evidence that the Spanish warships were firing their boilers. As the *New York* steamed away from the squadron, an officer aboard the *Brooklyn*, the flagship of Sampson's second in command, Commodore Winfield Scott Schley, thought he could see the smoke columns moving toward the harbor entrance.

"Afterbridge, there," the officer called out. "Report to the Commodore! The enemy's ships are coming out!"

Unable to persuade Cervera, General Blanco had finally ordered him to sea. Cervera's flagship, the cruiser *Maria Teresa*, cleared the harbor

Winfield Scott Schley played a key role in the sea battle of Santiago. *(Library of Congress, Prints & Photographs Division [LC-USZ62-121092])*

shortly after 9 o'clock. The cruiser's captain, Víctor Concas y Palau, ordered the bugles blown to signal the start of the action. Like his admiral, Concas had no confidence in the outcome. The sharp notes saddened rather than stirred him. "The sound of my bugles was the last echo of those which history tells us were sounded at the capture of Granada," Concas wrote. "It was the signal that the history of four centuries of grandeur was at an end and that Spain was becoming a nation of the fourth class."

Alarm gongs sounded throughout the American squadron. The ships cleared for action and the men hurried to their battle stations. The Spanish cruisers emerged in single file, spaced at intervals of 600 yards: the flagship, then *Vizcaya, Cristóbal Colón* and *Oquendo,* then two destroyers, *Plutón* and *Furor.* The Associated Press correspondent George Graham reported from the bridge of the *Brooklyn:*

> We saw what probably has not been witnessed since the days of the Armada, ships coming out for deadly battle, but dressed as for a regal parade or a festal day. From their shining black hulls, with huge golden figureheads bearing the crest and coat-of-arms of Spain, to the tops of their masts where fluttered proudly the immense silken flags, to the brightly colored awnings over their decks, they bespoke luxury and chivalry, and a proud defiance.

Capt. John Philip, the commanding officer of the battleship *Texas,* reached for a livelier image. "The Spanish ships came out as gaily as brides to the altar," he recalled. "Handsome vessels they certainly were, and with flags enough flying for a celebration parade." Still, the flags could not conceal the ships' deficiencies. Their bottoms were foul with marine growth, which substantially reduced their speed. For some reason, Cervera had not seen to the removal of wooden decks and ornaments, which greatly increased the risk of fire. The Spanish cruisers came out of the harbor at five knots and swung to the right, parallel to the shoreline, steering for the *Brooklyn.*

"Commodore, they are coming right at us," one of the *Brooklyn's* officers shouted.

"Well," Schley answered, "go right at them."

Already some miles to the east, Sampson, aboard the *New York,* heard the warning gun and ordered the ship to turn about and head back for Santiago. Sampson could see most of the developing action, but the *New*

American warships pound Admiral Cervera's cruisers off Santiago, July 3, 1898. *(National Archives)*

York trailed too far away for him to influence it. He had, however, left behind a general tactical plan in the event of a Spanish breakout: the Americans, from their blockade stations in an eight-mile-long arc off Santiago, were to rush the harbor entrance as the enemy emerged. But the Spanish managed to get out of the harbor before the American warships could converge on them. The battle thus developed into a chase on parallel lines, the Americans straining to close the distance. The *Maria Teresa* opened fire first.

"I remember very distinctly seeing the jets of water ahead and astern; and over and short; and the roar of the projectiles was one of the things that can be heard once in a lifetime," Schley wrote. "The thought passed through my mind that after all our precautions and waiting, those fellows would get away." The Americans returned a heavy fire, concentrating on the *Maria Teresa.* Soon her wooden decks were ablaze, costing Cervera his chance to escape. The *Iowa, Texas,* and *Brooklyn,* pouring on coal, were gradually catching up. A shell pierced a steam pipe, filling the

Maria Teresa's aft turret with hot steam and scalding several gunners to death.

The Spanish gunners were off their mark. "They fired high at first," Capt. Henry Taylor of the battleship *Indiana* reported. "I could hear, from the *Indiana*'s bridge, the screech and hum of many shells passing over our heads." Smoke hung thickly over the sea, blackening and blinding lookouts, range-finders, and gun captains. The Spanish were hidden from view for several minutes at a time. "One had the sensation of standing up against an unseen foe, the most disagreeable sensation in warfare," wrote Captain Philip of the *Texas*.

The little Spanish destroyers were the last to leave the shelter of Santiago harbor. The U.S. gunboat *Gloucester,* a converted yacht (the financier J. P. Morgan's *Corsair*), hurried to intercept the enemy light vessels. Soon the battleships opened fire on them. A large shell from the *Iowa* seemed to cut the *Furor* in two. "Then she swung slowly around and disappeared," Capt. Robley Evans of the *Iowa* reported. Several hits drove the *Plutón* onto the rocks.

Sampson and the *New York* reached the fringe of the battle in time to witness the final moments of the Spanish destroyers. *Brooklyn* and *Oregon* were away to the west, pouring a rapid fire into *Maria Teresa.* The Spanish flagship dropped out of the line, ablaze. Cervera ordered her to run for shore. "I steered for a small beach west of Punta Cabrera, where we ran aground just as the engines stopped," he wrote. "In this painful situation, when explosions commenced to be heard in the ammunition rooms, I gave orders to lower the flag and flood all the magazines." By then, fire had spread throughout the stricken ship.

The U.S. ships turned their full attention to the next vessel in the Spanish line, the *Oquendo.* Evans recalled:

> She rolled and staggered like a drunken thing, and finally seemed to stop her engines. I thought she was going to strike her colors, and was on the point of ordering the battery to cease firing, when she started ahead again and we redoubled our efforts to sink her. As I looked at her I could see the shot holes come in her sides and our shells explode inside of her, but she pluckily held on her course and smothered us with a shower of shells and machine-gun shots.

The *Oquendo* ended up on the beach, too, aground a half-mile west of the *Maria Teresa.* The *Brooklyn, Oregon,* and *Iowa* overtook the

Vizcaya, originally the second ship in the Spanish line, and began to pummel it. "We could see men's bodies hurled into the air, and see others dropping over the sides," the Associated Press's Graham wrote. After a few minutes, a 13-inch shell from the *Oregon* found its target and the *Vizcaya* seemed to shudder from end to end. "Cheer after cheer rang through the ship, and our gunfire increased in rapidity," one of the *Oregon's* officers remembered. "The *Vizcaya* was on fire and heading for the shore!" At about 11:00, less than two hours after the start of the battle, the third Spanish cruiser ran aground and hauled her colors.

Only the *Cristóbal Colón* remained, but she had opened up a six-mile lead. The *Brooklyn* steered to try to head her off while the battleships edged in to force the Spanish vessel closer to shore. Below, in hellish heat, the stokers worked furiously to feed the boilers. Seaman R. Cross wrote in his diary:

> The poor men in the fire-room was working like horses, and to cheer them up we passed the word down the ventilators how things was going on, and they passed the word back if we would cut them down they would get us to where we could do it. So we settled down for a good chase for the *Colón* I thought she was going to run a way from us. But she had to make a curv and we headed for a point that she had to come out at.

The Americans gained steadily. At a few minutes before 1 P.M., the *Oregon* opened fire from extreme range, around 10,000 yards, launching a 1,100-pound projectile from one of the 13-inch guns in the forward turret. The big guns fired deliberately for several minutes. The sixth shot fell just ahead of the fleeing Spanish cruiser. As the *Colón* turned for shore, another heavy shell struck under its stern.

"Immediately her colors dropped in a heap at the foot of the flagstaff," an eyewitness aboard the *Oregon* reported. "The bugle sounded, 'Cease firing!'" The American crews cheered wildly. When American officers boarded the *Colón,* they found 15 feet of water in the engine room and all the valves open to let in the sea. The ship's senior officers were quietly taking a meal, and several of the crewmen were drunk.

As the *Iowa* approached the *Vizcaya,* Captain Evans could see Spanish sailors standing on a sandspit near their grounded ship, the water reaching their armpits. "The Cuban insurgents had opened fire on them

A wrecked Spanish cruiser aground near Santiago, July 3, 1898
(National Archives)

from the shore, and with a glass I could see plainly the bullets snipping the water up among them," Evans recalled. "The sharks, made ravenous by the blood of the wounded, were attacking them from the outside." Small American boats rescued the captain and surviving crewmen. Not long afterward, the *Vizcaya*'s forward magazine exploded, sending up a column of smoke that could be seen 15 miles away.

The *Gloucester* picked up Admiral Cervera and other survivors of the derelict *Maria Teresa*. A small boat brought Cervera off the beach and delivered him, dripping wet in his underwear, to Captain Evans in the *Iowa*.

The American ships reported one fatality, a sailor aboard the *Brooklyn*. The Spanish lost 323 men dead, 151 wounded, and 1,813 taken prisoner. There could be no doubt about the decisiveness of the victory. Claim for it, however, became a matter of fierce dispute. After the *Colón* had struck its colors, Commodore Schley signaled Admiral Sampson in the *New York*: "A glorious victory has been achieved. Details later." Schley expected a word of congratulation. Instead, Sampson replied with a terse "Report your casualties."

Sampson had observed the battle from a distance, but he believed his position as commander of the squadron entitled him to credit for the outcome. Besides, the tactical plan, such as it was, had been his. Schley had been the senior officer present at the onset of the battle. He felt the laurels belonged to him, even though he had hardly issued an order during the long fight with the Spanish cruisers.

Schley had a bitter grasp of naval realities. "If the battle had miscarried," he wrote later, "there would have been no difficulty whatever about who was in command, or who would have had to bear the censure." The evening after the battle, Schley sent an officer to the cable office at Siboney, the Cuban town near Daiquirí. One of Sampson's aides followed in hot pursuit, intercepting Schley's message announcing the victory before it could be sent. "The fleet under my command offers the nation, as a Fourth of July present, the whole of Cervera's fleet," Sampson's substitute cable read. It did not mention Schley's name.

Shafter's troops, of course, had heard the distant boom of naval artillery from the trenches around Santiago. Cervera's fleet had drawn the Americans there. Now that it was destroyed, Shafter felt even less inclined to assault the Spanish fortifications. He chose to rely on the slow, steady pressure of a siege, hoping the Spanish would surrender before yellow fever could decimate his army.

8

THE
SANTIAGO SIEGE

American frontline troops could hear distant gunfire from the sea all through the morning of July 3. Later in the day, they learned the navy had won a great victory—at least the equal of the army's success on San Juan Heights. The news greatly eased Gen. William Shafter's anxieties. "Now that the fleet is destroyed, I believe the garrison will surrender and all we have to do is hang on where we are and very soon starve them out," he remarked to his second in command, Gen. Joseph Wheeler.

For the time being, though, the Spanish resisted Shafter's surrender demand, which had been sent early in the day, before the naval battle. They agreed to no more than a brief cease-fire that would allow women, children, and neutrals to leave before the Americans began the shelling of Santiago. The Spanish commander, José Torál (he had succeeded Gen. Arsenio Linares, who was wounded on San Juan Heights), still held out hope for relief from a 4,000-man infantry column marching toward Santiago from the west of Cuba.

Packing up such possessions as they could carry, the refugees poured out onto the El Caney road. The Americans observed the procession from the heights. "I could see the town's people moving about and the soldiers cooking their dinners," the Rough Rider Frank Knox wrote home. "Santiago is a pretty place. It seems a pity to lay it in ruins." The foreign consuls in the city persuaded Shafter to extend the July 3 truce through the afternoon of July 6, delaying the expected bombardment. Knox and the other American troops watched thousands of evacuees stream through the U.S. lines.

Cuban insurgent troops open fire from behind breastworks, summer, 1898. *(U.S. Military Academy, West Point, N.Y.)*

"All day along the hot, dusty road leading from Santiago to El Caney passed the long, white line," Lt. John J. Pershing of the Tenth Cavalry recalled. "Frail, hungry women carried a bundle of clothing, a parcel of food or an infant, while weak and helpless children trailed wearily at the skirts of their wretched mothers." Some 20,000 civilians placed themselves in the care of the Americans. Food, medicines, and shelter were lacking. El Caney was a country village of 300 or so houses. By the end of the first week in July it had become, in Stephen Crane's vivid phrase, a "vast parrot-cage of chattering refugees."

The Americans found further cause for complaint about their Cuban allies. The Spanish relief column brushed aside a force of Cuban insurgents guarding the western approach to Santiago and entered the besieged city. Though these reinforcements merely added to Torál's supply problem, the Americans reproached their allies for permitting them to pass. Shafter had similar troubles: along with his own troops and a large contingent of *insurrectos*, he now had the refugees to feed. To other alleged Cuban shortcomings, the Americans renewed the charge of ingratitude. Crane, who had written about the immigrant poor of America's cities, thought he understood why so many Americans took offense:

> Everybody knows that the kind of sympathetic charity which loves to be thanked is often grievously disappointed and wounded in tenement districts, where people often accept gifts as if their own property had turned up after a short absence. The Cubans accept our stores in something of this way.

While emissaries of Shafter and Torál continued their negotiations, U.S. troops experienced several anxious days in the trenches. "They were hanging to the crest of the San Juan hills by their teeth and finger-nails, and it seemed as though at any minute their hold would relax and they would fall," Richard Harding Davis wrote. Despite the energy-draining heat, the Rough Riders worked to strengthen their lines. A regular engineer officer took Theodore Roosevelt aside to explain that the Rough Riders' improvements were not "scientific." Roosevelt readily agreed. "I had never before seen a trench," he explained, "except for those we captured from the Spaniards." Regimental work parties were duly instructed in up-to-date techniques of trench engineering.

As the surrender talks went on in the days following July 3, the troops settled into a pattern of siege routine. The rains blew in more frequently: downpour, fierce sun, downpour. When storm clouds appeared, officers and men would strip, wrap their clothes in rubber ponchos and stand naked in the warm rain. With the sun's return, out came the clothes, filthy and stiff with dried sweat. ("I do not at all mind other men's clothes being offensive to me," one officer told Davis, "but when I cannot go to sleep on account of my own it grows serious.") At sunset each day the regimental bands played the National Anthem. Then, in the hot, damp darkness, men arranged themselves as comfortably as they could in the half-drowned trenches. "It was not at all an unusual experience to sleep through the greater part of the night with the head lifted just clear of the water and the shoulder and one-half of the body down in it," Davis wrote.

For some reason Shafter had neglected to establish a supply depot near the front, so the army rarely had more than a 24-hour stockpile of food, coffee, and tobacco. As Roosevelt noted, the troops would soon have reached the point of starvation had a hurricane scattered the transports or a three-day rainstorm washed out the roads. There was nothing to forage; the Santiago environs had long since been picked clean. Davis wrote:

> For three years the land back of us toward Siboney had been successively swept by Cuban insurgents and Spanish columns. There was, in consequence, not a cow to give milk, nor even a hen to give eggs. There was not even a forgotten patch of potatoes or of corn. Mangoes, limes and running water was all that the country itself contributed to our support.

Roosevelt blamed the V Corps's commanding general for every deficiency. "It is criminal to keep Shafter in command," he wrote to his powerful friend Senator Henry Cabot Lodge. "He is utterly inefficient; and now he is panic struck. The mismanagement has been beyond belief. We are half-starved; and our men are sickening daily." Shafter's failures, Roosevelt insisted, had brought the expeditionary force to the verge of disaster.

Black U.S. troops pose during a peaceful interlude. Four regiments of black regulars fought in Cuba. *(National Archives)*

Rough Rider trenches overlooking Santiago, July 1898 *(National Archives)*

Conditions were immeasurably worse inside Santiago. The Spanish defenders were exhausted and sickly. Feverish soldiers could not be sent to the hospital—they were needed in the trench lines. Horses and cattle were starving for want of fodder. The men subsisted on a small amount of rice each day. "Unfortunately, the situation is desperate," wrote General Linares, who was recovering from his wound. "The surrender is imminent, otherwise we will only gain time to prolong an agony." But Torál found himself hindered, as Admiral Cervera had been, by the reluctance of Gen. Ramón Blanco in Havana to face the hard facts of a hopeless military situation.

Shafter repeated the surrender demand on July 6 and granted Torál another three days to consult Havana and Madrid. When Torál finally replied, he offered to evacuate Santiago if the Americans would let him march for Havana with all his weapons and equipment. Shafter forwarded the proposal to Washington, appending his recommendation in favor of acceptance and including a footnote that three cases of yellow fever had been reported among the U.S. troops at Siboney.

Russell Alger, the secretary of war, rejected Torál's proposal out of hand and instructed Shafter to consent to nothing short of unconditional surrender. President William McKinley followed up with a barbed message of his own. "What you went to Santiago for was the Spanish army," he lectured Shafter. "If you allow it to evacuate with its arms you must meet it somewhere else. This is not war." So the shelling and sharpshooting resumed, though without much intensity on either side.

The Invisible Killers

FOR EVERY AMERICAN WHO DIED IN BATTLE IN CUBA, disease claimed two. Yellow fever caused the greatest dismay; some U.S. commanders predicted the death rate in the expeditionary force could reach 50 percent. As it happened, malaria proved more disruptive. Racked with fever and chills, Gen. Joseph Wheeler, the cavalry division commander, had to be carried to the battlefront outside Santiago on a litter. All the same, it was the first confirmed cases of yellow fever in the U.S. lines on July 9, 1898, that sent waves of shock and fear through the army.

Yellow fever had been endemic in Cuba since 1650, and July and August historically were the worst months for outbreaks. Nobody knew how it spread, only that it could be fatal in 85 percent of the cases. With those first cases, the sick were isolated in a hospital camp at Siboney, along the southeast coast of Cuba. The authorities assigned an African-American regiment, the Twenty-fourth Infantry, to operate the camp on the grounds that blacks had a "special immunity" to tropical diseases. Over a six-week period, malaria or yellow fever claimed the lives of fully one-third of the regiment's 460 men.

With the end of hostilities came demands for the removal of the troops from infected areas. On August 2, the V Corps sick lists contained 4,290 names. Individual regiments reported as many as 200 cases of malaria. In Washington, the authorities hesitated, figuring the army might have to resume fighting in Cuba. Then senior volunteer officers took the initiative, publicizing the army's plight in letters leaked to the Associated Press. "To keep us here, in the opinion of every officer commanding a division or a brigade, will simply involve the destruction of thousands," one of the letters read. The resultant outcry led to immediate action. Transports began loading troops for home on August 7, only five days after the letter's publication.

The frontline troops of both armies sometimes arranged tacit truces; there were few casualties in the trenches from gunshots during these steamy July days. In the rear, however, the Spanish guerrillas continued to harass American lines of communication. They fired on mule trains, at medical corpsmen and doctors, even at chaplains. Taking matters into his own hands, Roosevelt sent out a detail of Rough Riders to flush one especially effective group of Spanish snipers. The Americans were "first-class woodsmen and mountain men who were also good shots," Roosevelt explained. "They started systematically after them, and showed themselves much superior to the guerrillas' own game." Within a day or two, the Rough Rider irregulars had killed 11 guerrillas.

With the Spanish stalling and fever spreading through the camps, Shafter again asked the U.S. Navy to force an entrance into Santiago harbor. As before, Adm. William Sampson refused, citing danger from mines and shore batteries. Finally, at daybreak on July 11, U.S. artillery opened on the besieged city. At midday, Shafter declared another truce and sent yet another surrender demand through the Spanish lines. In this one, he tendered a U.S. government offer to ferry the Spanish forces home to Spain, free of charge, in return for unconditional surrender.

Shafter and Gen. Nelson Miles, the army commander in chief, met Torál between the lines on July 13. "I told him that we offered him liberal terms, namely, to return his troops to Spain," Miles wrote. "He said that under Spanish law he was not permitted to surrender as long as he had ammunition and food, and that he must maintain the honor of Spanish arms." Miles gave Torál until noon of the following day to think matters over.

Torál replied before the deadline: He would surrender, he told Shafter and Miles, contingent on the approval of the government in Madrid. To Shafter's surprise, Torál included not just the troops defending Santiago but all the forces in his territorial command—some 12,000 men in several garrisons outside Santiago, all of them beyond the Americans' reach. Two days of tedious negotiations over details followed. The formal ceremonies were scheduled for July 17, a Sunday.

Shafter and the other senior American officers, with a cavalry escort, met Torál and his entourage in an open field outside Santiago. The generals exchanged the customary courtesies. "The Spanish troops then presented arms," General Wheeler recalled, "and the Spanish flag, which for three hundred and eighty-two years had floated over the city, was pulled

U.S. troops react to word of the Spanish surrender at Santiago, July 1898. *(National Archives)*

down and furled forever." Wheeler was keenly observant as the column passed through the Spanish defensive works. He wrote:

> As we rode for the first time into Santiago we were struck by the excellent manner in which the Spanish lines were intrenched, and more especially by the formidable defenses with which they had barricaded roads. It would indeed have been a hard task for American troops, were they ever so brave and courageous, to have taken a city by storm which was protected by such defenses as these.

The Americans found a picturesque city of narrow streets, low-built stucco houses and massive stone public buildings mottled with tropical damp. In the Cathedral Plaza were the governor's palace and—for rest, refreshment and the news of the moment—the Café Venus. The U.S. flag rose over the governor's palace, 21 guns were fired in salute, and the band of the Sixth Infantry struck up the patriotic song "Hail, Columbia." In the ancient cathedral, vespers were chanted as usual that evening. One of the newspaper correspondents reported hearing an old priest praying for the success of Spanish arms; he was too late. The next day, Spanish diplomats in Paris approached the French government about trying to arrange an armistice that would end the war.

The refugees returned to Santiago— "an endless squalid procession," in Roosevelt's words—from El Caney and the other outlying camps. Some of the Rough Riders tried to assist the women and children by offering food or volunteering to carry their scant possessions. Roosevelt put a stop to that, fearing that his men would contract diseases.

Now that the fighting had ended, the real enemy appeared. By late July more than 4,000 men—20 percent of the American expeditionary force—had fallen sick, mostly from malaria and heat exhaustion. "We saw that their faces were yellow, their eyes drawn, their cheeks hollow and sunken, their skin dry and crackling like parchment," the correspondent Stephen Bonsal wrote. With the rest of the cavalry division, the Rough Riders came out of the line and went into camp in the foothills west of El Caney. They were as hard-hit by fever as any other unit, but Roosevelt and his officers, after inspecting the big field hospital, had decided the sick would stand a better chance of recovery in camp. There were no cots and few medicines. An officer described the scene:

> The men answering surgeons' calls would get salts one morning and the next castor oil. It was no strange sight, at reveille, to see men crawl out of their tents, try to stand up but fall like logs before anyone could reach them. This was one of the stages of malaria. Home sickness was another, and perhaps the worst feature we had to deal with. With nothing to do the men had plenty of time to think. This is what wrought the mischief. A soldier must not think. The men who tried the hardest to keep up, in most cases, were the best off.

The great dread was yellow fever, but in fact most of the cases were malarial—less certainly fatal but debilitating nevertheless. "The lithe college athletes had lost their spring," Roosevelt recalled. "The tall, gaunt hunters and cow-punchers lounged listlessly in their dog-tents, which were steaming morasses during the torrential rains, and then ovens when the sun blazed down." In the course of a few weeks in Cuba, Roosevelt's orderly, Henry Bardshar, lost 80 pounds.

The troops were issued rations of fresh meat for the first time in five weeks on July 22, five days after the Spanish surrender. Standard fare

A fever-stricken U.S. soldier is removed from an ambulance. *(National Archives)*

continued to be bacon, hard bread, sugar, and coffee, and these rarely in sufficient quantities. Expert opinion supported Roosevelt's assessment. "The men uniformly appear weak, enervated, tired—need as near absolute rest as possible, and change to a cooling and nourishing diet," the cavalry division's inspector general reported.

The War Department intended to keep V Corps in Santiago as an occupation force; after all, thousands of Spanish troops remained at large in Cuba, and the United States and Spain were still formally at war. Also, there were strong political pressures against returning an army infected with yellow fever to the United States. Even so, Shafter urged an immediate evacuation. "If it is not done," he cabled the War Department, "I believe the death-rate will be appalling." Already the mournful tones of Taps were too often heard. Pvt. Charles Post of the Seventy-first New York wrote:

> Each morning, we would hear bugles blowing Taps very shortly after reveille. First, from far off in the hills back of the trench line, a volley—the burial detail. Then the bugle. The sickness was striking in harder. The volleys became more frequent and one bugle followed another throughout the day; they followed each other almost as if they were but echoes among the hills about us.

At the end of July, Shafter called a council of senior officers to plot a response to the crisis. The officers decided to send a "round-robin" letter, signed by all, asking the War Department for relief, and to have Roosevelt, now commanding one of the cavalry brigades, write a second letter describing conditions and deliver it to the Associated Press (AP) correspondent covering Shafter's headquarters. The AP dispatch would appear in newspapers across the United States, thereby building pressure to bring V Corps home. Regular officers, with their future careers to consider, could never risk such a scheme. As a volunteer, however, Roosevelt considered himself to be safe from War Department reprisal.

"This army must be moved at once, or perish," Roosevelt wrote. "As the army can be safely moved now, the persons responsible for preventing such a move will be responsible for the loss of many thousands of lives." The letter, published in American newspapers on August 2, created the hoped-for sensation. As it happened, the War Department already had determined to evacuate V Corps. Transports soon arrived off Santiago. By August 8 the first troops—among them, the Rough Riders—were en route to the newly established quarantine camp at Montauk, Long Island, 125 miles east of New York City.

By the third week of August, more than 20,000 men had been taken out of Cuba. Roosevelt and the Rough Riders reached Montauk in reasonably good condition after an uneventful voyage. "I was myself in first-class health, all the better for having lost twenty pounds," Roosevelt reported. After a few days of confusion, the camp began to run smoothly. "The men lived high," Roosevelt went on, "with milk, eggs, oranges and any amount of tobacco."

Not everyone was so fortunate. More than 500 men had died of fever or some other tropical disease in Cuba—twice the number of battle fatalities. Another 250 died in camp at Montauk. Many of the survivors never recovered their full health. Dr. Nicholas Senn, the chief surgeon of the U.S. Volunteers, left this summary:

Those who saw the different regiments leave our State and national camps would find it difficult to recognize and identify the soldiers of the Cuban campaign. The men left in excellent spirits. Most of them returned as mere shadows of themselves. The pale faces, the sunken eyes, the staggering gait and the emaciated forms show only too plainly the effects of climate and disease. Many of them are wrecks for life, others are candidates for a premature grave, and hundreds will require the most careful attention and treatment before they regain the vigor they lost in Cuba.

The war had ended for V Corps, but it continued for two other American expeditionary forces. The first U.S. troops reached the distant Philippines in late June. Reinforced in July, they were preparing to attack Spanish positions around Manila. Meanwhile, Gen. Nelson Miles received authorization to sail for Puerto Rico on July 18, the same day the Spanish had put out the first peace feelers through their ambassador in Paris. Still, Miles had every expectation of having to fight for the Caribbean island. He decided to land his 3,400-man invasion force near Ponce, in the southwest corner of Puerto Rico, and march overland for the capital, San Juan.

9

PUERTO RICO
AND THE PHILIPPINES

What had begun as an almost accidental crusade to avenge the sinking of the USS *Maine* now became a campaign to seize Spanish-owned colonies around the world. President William McKinley only mentioned Cuba upon the outbreak of war in April. Yet on July 25, sailors from the cruiser USS *Gloucester* were landing at Guánica, west of Ponce on the south coast of the island of Puerto Rico. A party of blue-jackets quickly accepted the surrender of the few Spanish policemen there and ran up the Stars and Stripes over the town. The small Spanish garrison fired several wild shots, then fled. The U.S. infantry, about 2,000 men from the Sixth Illinois and the Sixth Massachusetts Regiments, were conveyed from the transports and landed at quayside through the day. By evening, Gen. Nelson Miles had established a secure lodgement in Guánica.

The townspeople seemed to take the invasion in stride, while the commonplace sights of the sleepy little port charmed their conquerors. "To those of us who had just come from Santiago," wrote Richard Harding Davis, still in pursuit of a good story, "the sight of the women sitting on porches and rocking in bent-wood chairs, the lighted swinging lamps with cut-glass pendants, and the pictures and mirrors on the walls which we saw that night through the open doors seemed part of some long-forgotten existence." The troops camped on the verges of a single long street that led inland from the harbor and awaited word to advance.

General Miles prepared a complicated campaign plan to overwhelm the 8,000 demoralized Spanish regulars, supplemented by some 9,000 poorly armed militiamen, in Puerto Rico. A Civil War veteran (he had been Confederate president Jefferson Davis's jailer at Fortress Monroe, Virginia, from 1865–67) and a famous Indian fighter, Miles had risen to become commanding general of the U.S. Army in 1895. He seems to have viewed the Puerto Rico expedition as an opportunity to demonstrate his mastery of the art of generalship. Miles meant to show the world that at least one American commander could find an alternative to the type of plodding, messy siege warfare that General William Shafter had waged in Cuba.

Part of the Greater Antilles island chain, Puerto Rico is 108 miles long and about 40 miles wide, with a total land area of 3,400 square miles. A mountain spine runs east to west for the full length of the island. In 1898, Puerto Rico had only one modern road, a 70-mile-long military highway running southwest to northeast and linking Ponce, the largest city, with San Juan, the capital. The island's 950,000 inhabitants

A battery of the Fourth U.S. Artillery shells a Spanish blockhouse near Coamo, Puerto Rico, August 1898. *(National Archives)*

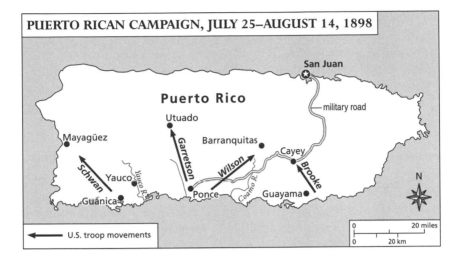

PUERTO RICAN CAMPAIGN, JULY 25–AUGUST 14, 1898

sustained themselves by producing sugarcane, rice, and corn. Unlike Cuba, 500 miles to the west, Puerto Rico enjoyed a relatively dry, healthy climate; Americans here ran less risk of disease. Unlike Cuba, Puerto Rico had mounted no significant challenge to Spanish colonial rule. Some Puerto Ricans had campaigned for local autonomy, however, and Spain had granted the island home rule in November 1897, as part of the broader package of reforms aimed at quelling the Cuban outbreak.

With Guánica secure, American troops came ashore at other points on the island. General Miles formed four separate columns to converge on San Juan from four different directions. On July 26, detachments of the Sixth Illinois and the Sixth Massachusetts fought a brief skirmish with the Spanish at Yauco on the Ponce road. After the Americans brushed this small force aside, the Spanish garrison at Ponce withdrew, leaving the city undefended. Ponce welcomed the occupying Americans with processions, music, and red, white, and blue banners draped from the balconies. "Long live Washington!" one man called out, in English.

Miles expressed complete satisfaction with the islanders' attitude. "At least four-fifths of the people hail with great joy the arrival of United States troops," he cabled the War Department. "They are bringing in transportation, beef cattle and other supplies. Volunteers are surrendering themselves with arms and ammunition." The Americans camped in the plaza and along the residential streets of Ponce. They again marveled at the Puerto Ricans' ability to carry on with life as usual. "Milkmen appeared at dawn," Irving Ruland, a trooper in a New York volunteer cavalry contingent, wrote home. "The milkmen milked the cows at the doorsteps directly into small-necked bottles."

Successive landings built the American force to a total of 15,000 men. After a week's preparation, Miles ordered his four columns to begin their cross-island march toward San Juan.

The campaign had some of the feel of summer maneuvers. "This is a prosperous and beautiful county," Miles cabled Secretary of War Russell Alger. "The army will soon be in mountain region; weather delightful; troops in best of health and spirits; anticipate no insurmountable obstacles in future results." Rumors of an armistice began to circulate. "I am not bloodthirsty," one staff officer, hearing them, wrote to his wife, "but I should like to see a little real fighting after all the farce."

The first serious skirmishes took place on August 9, on the Ponce–San Juan road. The Spanish rear guards lost 40 dead before retreating. Miles's westernmost column lost one man killed and 16 wounded in a firefight south of Mayagüez on August 10. American troops occupied Mayagüez the following day. Then, late on August 12, Miles learned that the United States and Spain had signed a peace protocol.

In response, Miles ordered a halt to all offensive operations. The six engagements of the Puerto Rican campaign cost the United States seven men killed and 36 wounded. The Spanish reported some 450 casualties. The brief American campaign went down at home as a lark. Through no particular fault of his own, General Miles had found himself unable to conclusively demonstrate his military prowess. But correspondent Davis entered the lists as Miles's champion. He had not forgotten General Shafter's insults during the Daiquirí landings, and praise for Shafter's rival could be a satisfying form of revenge. "Anyone who has seen a really great matador face a bull in a bull-ring has certainly thought that the man had gained his reputation easily," Davis wrote. "The reason the Spanish bull gored our men in Cuba and failed to touch them in Puerto Rico was entirely due to the fact that Miles was an expert matador."

By the second week of August, the American flag floated over most of Puerto Rico. On the other side of the world, meanwhile, American forces had seized the tiny Pacific island outpost of Guam and, with Filipino insurgents under Emilio Aguinaldo, were preparing to close the ring around Manila, the capital of the Philippine archipelago.

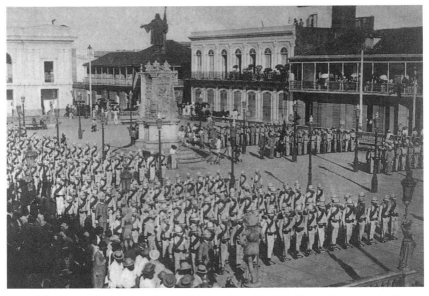

Spanish troops form up to leave Mayagüez, Puerto Rico. *(National Archives)*

The cruiser *Charleston,* escorting the troop transports, had opened fire on Spanish positions on Guam on June 20. When a landing party from the *Charleston* came ashore to demand surrender, the sailors found that the Spanish had no idea a war was on, as no ship had called at the island since mid-April. The Americans rounded up the Spanish garrison, left a small occupation force behind, and steamed on toward the Philippines.

Commodore George Dewey enforced a strict blockade of Manila after the destruction of the Spanish squadron on May 1. Spanish forces posed little problem for Dewey, but a German naval squadron that turned up to "observe" American operations had kept him in a constant state of irritation for several weeks. The Germans ignored the blockade, steaming in and out of Manila Bay whenever they chose, and even sent landing parties ashore for discussions with the Spanish defenders.

In a series of stiff protests, Dewey accused the Germans of interfering in American affairs and of harassing the Filipino insurgents. At one point, his patience exhausted, Dewey threatened to open fire on the German warships. His aggressive response gained broad support at home, even if one newspaper did feel bound to remind its readers that the

Aguinaldo and the Americans

THE UNITED STATES MISREAD EMILIO AGUINALDO AND his insurgency. American diplomatic and military officials either discounted the Philippine leader or failed entirely to recognize him as a shaper of events. Either way, the results were tragic, particularly for Filipinos.

"In spite of all statements to the contrary, I know [the insurgents] are fighting for annexation to the U.S. first and for independence second if the U.S. decides to decline," wrote Rounseville Wildman, the American consul in Hong Kong. In Manila, Adm. George Dewey—a sailor, after all, not a diplomat—took Wildman's assessment at face value.

Aguinaldo returned to the Philippines from exile in Hong Kong aboard a U.S. warship, landing at Cavite near Manila on May 19, 1898. Members of a Senate committee in 1902 asked Dewey why he permitted Aguinaldo to come ashore. "I let him come over as an act of courtesy," he responded, "just as you sometimes give money to a man to get rid of him."

Later, Aguinaldo insisted that Dewey all but promised him the U.S. would guarantee Philippine independence—"America needs no colonies," Dewey reportedly said. So perhaps Aguinaldo labored under a misapprehension of American intentions when he issued a series of independence proclamations for the islands. The first declaration caught the befogged Dewey unawares.

"That was the first intimation; the first I had ever heard of the independence of the Philippines," Dewey told the Senate committee. "I never dreamed they wanted independence."

Monroe Doctrine, asserting U.S. primacy in the Americas, "did not apply to the universe." The Germans eventually withdrew, and Dewey's burdens were considerably eased with the arrival in late June of the first contingent of American infantry. By the end of the month, the American commander, Gen. Wesley Merritt, had 11,000 troops ashore and ready to advance on Manila.

Aguinaldo's insurgents had already done much of the work for the Americans, having cleared Cavite Province of Spaniards and besieging Manila. Emboldened by these military achievements, Aguinaldo proclaimed Philippine independence in mid-June and formed a civil government shortly thereafter. At first, Dewey treated the insurgents as helpful allies, as they certainly were. Years later, he insisted that he had given the Aguinaldo revolutionaries no grounds to believe they and the Americans were in partnership against the Spanish. He let Aguinaldo come to Manila "as an act of courtesy, just as you sometimes give money to a man to get rid of him; not that I expected anything from them," Dewey wrote. On instructions from Washington, Dewey refused to recognize the insurgents' claims. When sufficient American forces had arrived, Merritt made preparations to replace the Filipinos in the trenches outside Manila with his own units.

Gen. Wesley Merritt led troops into Manila in the final battle with the Spanish for control of the Philippines. *(Library of Congress, Prints & Photographs Division [LC-B8172-1830])*

A view of Emilio Aguinaldo's camp 60 miles north of Manila.
(Library of Congress, Prints & Photographs Division [LC-USZ62-126667])

So the Filipinos were pushed aside; U.S. troops moved into the insurgents' lines on the night of July 29. Two nights later, the Spanish opened an intensive cannonade supported by musketry. After 90 minutes of furious action, 50 Americans had fallen, including 10 who were killed. There were briefer exchanges on several successive nights. Then the Spanish commander, Gen. Fermín Jaudenes y Alvarez, let it be known that he would put up no more than a token defense of Manila—as Dewey explained, "to show a form of resistance for the sake of Spanish honor." The Americans sent the first surrender demand to the Spanish on August 6, the same day that Aguinaldo, who had no intention of going away, published another declaration of independence and issued an appeal to the European powers for recognition of a Philippine republic.

Jaudenes set two conditions for the surrender of Manila: The Americans would stage a sham battle, and they would under no circumstances allow insurgent forces into the city. Dewey and Merritt readily agreed. They would launch a real attack; the Spanish would respond with a real defense; then, after a decent interval, the defenders would hoist the white flag.

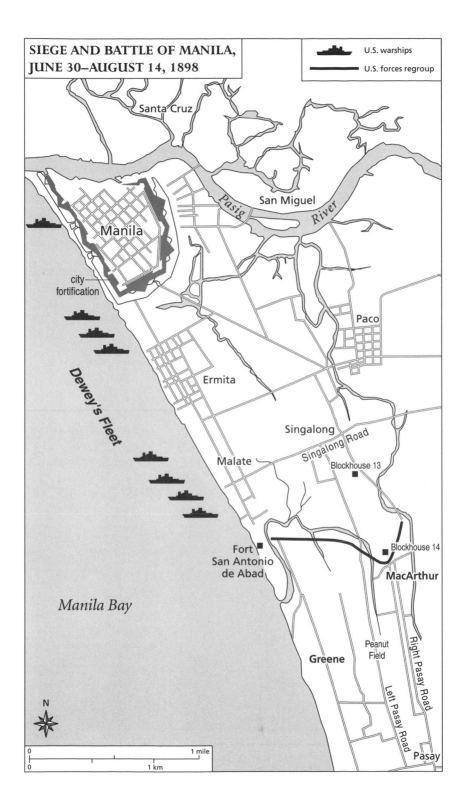

U.S. troops stand on ramparts at Manila. *(Library of Congress, Prints & Photographs Division [LC-D401-21488])*

Dewey's warships commenced the affair at 9:30 A.M. on August 13, with a bombardment of Fort San Antonio, an outlying Spanish defensive work. "Jaudenes said his honor demanded that," Dewey noted. "So I had to fire, to kill a few people." Two infantry brigades advanced through fields and along the beach toward Manila. Finding the fort abandoned, the foot soldiers pushed on down the Camino Real, the main road into the city. Reporter Frank Davis Millet described the scene:

> The broad, straight thoroughfare was now busy with our men dashing across by squads from one side to the other and peppering the retreating Spaniards whenever they caught sight of them. Now they climbed into the garden of a pleasant villa, now they dodged among the plantains and behind the wattled fences of the native huts, always advancing and firing. Deliberately and stubbornly the scattered enemy retired from corner to corner, from cover to cover, pausing only to pump out bullets as they went.

There were casualties in this "mock battle"—six men killed and more than 40 wounded on the American side. Finally, from the bridge of the *Olympia,* Dewey spotted a white flag flying from a bastion of one of the Spanish forts. Brig. Gen. Francis Greene, leading one of the infantry columns, marched down to the captain of the port's office, ordered the Spanish flag hauled down, and raised the Stars and Stripes in its place. The firing died away.

Dewey and Merritt observed the letter of their agreement with General Jaudenes. American units met insurgent Filipino troops pushing up close to the city. "Strong guards were posted," Merritt wrote, "and General Aguinaldo was given to understand that no insurgents would be allowed to enter with arms." Within a few days, explicit orders arrived from Washington: There would be no joint American-insurgent occupation of Manila.

Dewey, Merritt and Jaudenes signed the formal documents surrendering Manila on August 14. Two days later, the dispatch boat from Hong Kong steamed in with word that the war between the United States and Spain had ended. The sham battle, it turned out, actually had been fought a day after peace had come.

The Spanish regent, María Cristina, had sent out the first peace feelers toward the end of July, not long after the surrender of Santiago. The Spanish offered Cuba in return for peace, but sought to retain possession of Puerto Rico, Guam, and the Philippines. President McKinley asked for Spanish evacuation of Cuba, cession of Puerto Rico and Guam to the United States, and U.S. occupation of Manila and its environs until the signing of the peace treaty that would determine the final fate of the Philippines. In a note that reached McKinley on August 9, the Spanish accepted the American terms.

On August 12, at 4:30 in the afternoon, Secretary of State William R. Day and the French ambassador, Jules Cambon, acting for Spain, signed the peace protocol in Washington. In the following weeks, in the crowded insurgent camps outside steamy Manila, anger, disappointment, and a sense of betrayal began to build toward a flashpoint that threatened to touch off another war.

10

THE BATTLE
FOR EMPIRE

"It has been a splendid little war; begun with the highest motives, carried on with magnificent intelligence and spirit, favored by that fortune which loves the brave," John Hay, the American ambassador in London, wrote to his friend Theodore Roosevelt toward the end of July. But even in 1898 there were a few dissenters from Hay's assessment. "We cannot expect again to have an enemy so entirely unapt as Spain showed herself to be," Alfred Thayer Mahan, the philosopher of sea power, warned his self-applauding countrymen.

The Spanish-American War *had* been little, if not entirely splendid; Spain had not proven to be a very dangerous adversary, as adversaries go. The United States suffered 379 battle deaths—10 sailors, 369 soldiers. (Altogether, 5,000 U.S. servicemen died of disease or other noncombat causes in 1898.) To the families of the dead, of course, the price of victory was heartbreakingly dear. Still, the McKinley administration could view the losses as light, particularly in comparison to the gains. By the autumn of 1898, Spain was preparing to leave Cuba; the United States would claim, by right of conquest, much of what remained of the Spanish Empire.

Already, though, opposition to overseas territorial acquisition had begun to stir. After several years of hesitation, the United States annexed the nominally independent Hawaiian Islands in early July 1898. President William McKinley tried to quiet the skeptics with the claim that another rising Pacific power might take Hawaii if the United States did not. "We cannot let these islands go to Japan," the president told Senator

George Hoar, a Massachusetts Republican who had emerged as a leader of the opposition to American expansionist policy. McKinley signed the joint congressional resolution annexing Hawaii on July 7. Believing that the Hawaiians themselves endorsed the new connection, Hoar went along, reluctantly.

The United States had long been involved in Hawaii. The Philippines were another matter. Positions on both sides were firm. "Where the flag once goes up it must never come down," declared Henry Cabot Lodge, the other Republican senator from Massachusetts and a leading imperialist. McKinley decided the United States should keep all it held, at least until the conclusion of a treaty with Spain; after that, the president thought, the United States should keep as much as it wanted. Influential newspapers, business groups and missionary societies supported annexation. But opposition had become increasingly vocal. Anti-imperialist resolutions were adopted at mass meetings around the country. "Is the commandment 'Thou shalt not steal' qualified by the proviso 'unless it is necessary'?" one orator asked an audience at Faneuil Hall in Boston, neatly encapsulating the chief argument of the anti-imperialists.

With the armistice, the United States began to demobilize its hastily assembled volunteer army. To the volunteers, the process moved at a painfully slow pace. "The signing of the protocol with the Spaniards brought us great trouble," recalled an officer of an infantry division in camp near Lexington, Kentucky. "The men had volunteered for the war and now that the war was over they could see no reason why they should not lay down their guns anywhere they happened to be and walk home. As many as three hundred men would be reported absent without leave from a single regiment." The War Department began dismantling the volunteer units as early as August 24—less than two weeks after the cease-fire.

In camp at Montauk Point, Long Island, Roosevelt and the now-famous Rough Riders awaited their return to civilian life. "My regiment will be mustered out in a few days, and then I shall be footloose," Roosevelt wrote to a friend. "Just at the moment there is vociferous popular demand to have me nominated for governor, but I very gravely question whether it materializes." It did, of course; Roosevelt would win the New York governorship in November, a long step on his road to the White House.

The four-month life of the First U.S. Volunteer Cavalry came rambunctiously to a close. "A former populist candidate for Attorney-

Rough Riders waited for formal dismissal from their duties at Montauk Point in New York. *(Library of Congress, Prints & Photographs Division [LC-USZ62-92485])*

General in Colorado delivered a fervent oration in favor of free silver," Roosevelt recalled. "A number of the college boys sang; but most of the men gave vent to their feelings by improvised dances." The Rough Riders were formally disbanded at Montauk on September 15.

Despite some initial problems, Montauk proved to be one of the healthier army camps. At Chickamauga, near Chattanooga, Tennessee, more than 400 men died of disease after the fighting had ended overseas. Those who remained were restless, depressed, eager to go home. Newspapers took up the common soldiers' cause, thundering against War Department maladministration. Camp epidemics, claims of cheating on government contracts, and other alleged shortcomings were widely reported. The pressure grew so intense that Secretary of War Russell Alger asked for an independent commission to clear his reputation. The Dodge Commission, named for its chairman, the Civil War general and railroad builder Grenville Dodge, eventually found that there had been no dishonesty or intentional neglect, but a great deal of incompetence and mismanagement.

THE BATTLE FOR EMPIRE

The American Peace Commission, with McKinley's Ohio political crony and friend William R. Day in charge, sailed for France in mid-September. Negotiations began in Paris on October 1. American and Spanish diplomats haggled for several weeks over whether the United States would assume Spain's Cuban debts, the Spanish proposing to transfer some $400 million in obligations along with sovereignty of the island. The United States refused.

The other great issue was the Philippines. For several months, American policy had been tilting toward acquisition of the islands. McKinley considered the options: returning the islands to Spain, handing them over to French or German colonial administration, or leaving the Filipinos to govern themselves. In the end, the president chose a fourth option. "There was nothing left for us to do but take them all," McKinley wrote, "and to educate the Filipinos, and uplift and civilize and Christianize them, and by God's grace do the very best we could by

In the autumn of 1898, hospitals like this U.S. Army Third Division hospital at Camp Hamilton, Kentucky, were transition points for many soldiers returning from war. *(Library of Congress, Prints & Photographs Division [LC-USZ62-95039])*

The Anti-Imperialists

AN OUTSPOKEN OPPOSITION BELATEDLY GATHERED TO contest U.S. annexation of the Philippines. The Anti-Imperialist League, established in late 1898, challenged the McKinley administration's plan to absorb the islands on moral, economic, racial, and constitutional grounds.

No anti-imperialist raised a more powerful—and embittered—voice than the author Mark Twain, whose *Adventures of Huckleberry Finn* and other works made him one of the most widely read American novelists of the day. As Emilio Aguinaldo's insurrection neared an end in 1901, Twain savagely punctured American pretensions in an essay titled "The Philippine Incident":

> We are a World Power, no one can deny it. . . . We have bought some islands from a party who did not own them . . . we are indisputably in possession of a wide-spreading archipelago as if it were our property; we have pacified some thousands of the islanders and buried them; destroyed their fields, burned their villages, and turned their widows and orphans out of doors; subjugated the remaining ten millions by Benevolent Assimilation which is the pious new name of the musket."

Pretending to accept what he plainly regarded as the shameful logic of conquest, Twain went on:

> We are a World Power, we cannot get out of it now. . . . We realize, too late for escape, that we are the kind of World Power—for style and assets—that a prairie-dog village is, and that we cannot keep countenance when we try to look each other in the face; but no matter, we are in for it, and it is the duty of our Government to stand sentinel, with solemn mien, with lifted nose, and curved paws, on top of our little World Power-mound, and look out over the wide prairie; and if anything suspicious shows up on the horizon, bark.

Twain and his allies proved powerless to prevent the annexation. The United States ruled the Philippines as a colonial possession until 1946.

Mark Twain (Samuel Clemens) opposed the fighting between the United States and the Philippines on anti-imperialist grounds.
(Library of Congress, Prints & Photographs Division [LC-USZ62-112065])

them, as our fellow-men for whom Christ also died." On October 28, McKinley instructed the American commissioners to demand all of the Philippines as the price of a treaty.

The Spanish put up a stubborn diplomatic defense. They rejected the U.S. demand on November 4, arguing that the Americans actually had captured Manila *after* the peace protocol had been signed in Washington. Meanwhile, opposition to annexation was building rapidly in the United States. The newspaper baron Joseph Pulitzer campaigned against U.S. acquisition of the Philippines. In November, opponents of annexation formed the Anti-Imperialist League in Boston. Senator Hoar, the Civil War veteran and journalist Carl Schurz, and the steel baron Andrew Carnegie were among the founders. Authors Mark Twain and William Dean Howells, the social worker Jane Addams, former president Benjamin Harrison, and the presidents of Harvard and Stanford Universities were prominent anti-imperialists. The league's platform proclaimed:

> We hold that the policy known as imperialism is hostile to liberty and tends toward militarism. We regret that it has become necessary in the land of Washington and Lincoln to reaffirm that all men, of whatever race or color, are entitled to life, liberty and the pursuit of happiness. We insist that the subjugation of any people is "criminal aggression" and open disloyalty to the distinctive principles of our government.

The peace commissioners responded to the other side of the argument. "We have incurred a moral obligation to take all of the islands, govern them [and] civilize the natives," Commander R. B. Bradford, echoing the president, told the U.S. commissioners, and they pressed the claim to the Philippines. When the Spanish continued to resist, the Americans offered a cash gift of $20 million for cession of the islands. The Spanish reluctantly acquiesced, agreeing on November 28 to cede Cuba, Puerto Rico, Guam, and the Philippine archipelago. In their formal acceptance of the terms, the Spanish commissioners said:

> The Government of her Majesty . . . will not assume the responsibility of again bringing upon Spain all the horrors of war. In order to avoid them it resigns itself to the painful strait of submitting to the law of the victor, however harsh it may be, and as Spain lacks the material means to defend the rights she believes are hers, she accepts the only terms the United States offers her for the concluding of the treaty of peace.

Spanish forces formally surrender Havana, January 1, 1899. *(Library of Congress)*

The United States and Spain signed the Treaty of Paris on December 10, 1898. In Washington, the McKinley administration prepared for a difficult political battle in the Senate over ratification. Senator Hoar led the anti-annexation forces. Empire cut against the grain of the American tradition; it meant governing without the consent of the governed. Taking the Philippines, Hoar said, would make the United States "a cheapjack country, raking after the cart for the leavings of European tyranny."

Andrew Carnegie did not have a Senate vote, of course, but his immense steel fortune had long been at the service of the Republican Party and his defection especially worried McKinley and his allies. "He says the Administration will fall in irretrievable ruin the moment it shoots down one insurgent Filipino," John Hay wrote of Carnegie. Hay hardly exaggerated the steel baron's views. "Our young men volunteered to fight the oppressor," Carnegie declared. "I shall be surprised if they relish the work of shooting down the oppressed."

McKinley sent the treaty to the Senate on January 4, 1899. The debate was intense, bitter and exhausting. Hoar put the antiratification view simply: "I am willing to risk much for liberty," he said. "But I am willing to risk nothing for mere empire." Roosevelt stated his position with the brutal bluntness he reserved for his favorite political enemies. "It is difficult for me to speak with moderation of such men as Hoar," he said. "They are little better than traitors." One newspaper versifier expressed what had become a widely held notion with this lament:

> O Dewey at Manila
> That fateful first of May
> When you sank the Spanish squadron
> In almost bloodless fray,
> And gave your name to deathless fame;
> O glorious Dewey, say,
> Why didn't you weigh anchor
> And softly sail away?

From the islands, Gen. Wesley Merritt sounded a note of caution. Americans, he said, wrongly dismissed Filipinos as incapable of managing their own affairs. Ten thousand well-armed insurgents backed Aguinaldo's republic, and they were prepared to fight. With a new war, the $20 million the United States had paid for the islands might turn out to be a modest first installment only. As Representative Thomas Reed, the acerbic anti-imperialist Speaker of the House, put it, "We have bought ten million Malays at $2.00 a head unpicked, and nobody knows what it will cost to pick them." Relations between the Americans and the Filipinos went from bad to worse as the treaty terms became known and the Senate debate dragged on. Admiral George Dewey accused Aguinaldo of having a "big head." Aguinaldo accused the Americans of bad faith and continued to drill his insurgent army of 20 regiments. Aguinaldo's government controlled most of Manila's island, Luzon, as well as several other islands. Spanish garrisons held out in the larger towns, hanging on in order to surrender to U.S. forces as stipulated in the peace treaty. McKinley urged the American commanders in the Philippines to avoid open conflict with the insurgents. "They will come to see our benevolent purpose," he said. Still, tensions continued to rise. What now looks like the inevitable explosion occurred on the night of February 4, 1899.

Pacifying Ilocano Province

THE AMERICANS STYLED IT AN INSURRECTION; FOR Filipinos, it was a war for independence. As American casualties mounted in the campaign to "pacify" the Philippines, U.S. forces responded with increasing cruelty.

Veteran Daniel J. Evans testified about American interrogation methods in Ilocano Province to a U.S. Senate investigating committee in 1902. U.S. troops practiced the "water cure" on a guerrilla suspect who refused to reveal the whereabouts of his insurgent unit. A scout for the Americans grabbed the man by the head, jerked the head back, and poured water from a tomato can down his throat until he could hold no more.

"During this time one of the natives had a whip, about as large as my finger, and he struck him on the face and the bare back, and every time they would strike him it would raise a welt, and some blood would come," Evans went on. The captors forced more water into the insurgent, and when he could take no more they stuffed a gag in his mouth and tied him upright to a post.

Evans testified, "Then one man, an American soldier, who was over six feet tall, and who was very strong too, struck this native in the pit of the stomach as hard as he could strike him, just as rapidly as he could."

Did he break down and betray his comrades? asked one of the senators.

"I believe he did," said Evans, "because I didn't hear of any more water cure inflicted on him."

One Private Grayson of the First Nebraska Volunteers called out a challenge to a Filipino approaching his picket lines "I yelled 'Halt,'" Grayson explained later. "He immediately shouted 'Halto' at me. Well, I thought the best thing to do was to shoot him." Grayson and another infantryman brought down three insurgents and then returned to their outpost. "Line up fellows," Grayson told the Americans, "the niggers are in here all through these yards." Such slurs, reported by this naive soldier, expressed the attitude of many Americans toward the "natives" of these new, exotic possessions.

The Filipino insurgents opened a general offensive against U.S. forces the next day, February 5. The initial attacks were repulsed at a cost of

175 Americans killed and wounded. In Washington on February 6, the U.S. Senate voted 57-27 to ratify the Treaty of Paris, reaching the necessary two-thirds majority with only one vote to spare.

The easy successes of the Spanish-American War could not obscure the serious shortcomings of the U.S. military establishment. Organization and supply services were badly flawed. Medical services were primitive. The army's infantry fought well, but its artillery arm had almost no impact on battlefield events. The navy won two smashing victories against a weak enemy, but the sea battles exposed serious deficiencies in American ship design: the U.S. warships were too slow and too lightly armored. American marksmanship left a lot to be desired as well. The naval board of officers that examined the Spanish wrecks after the Santiago battle found evidence of only 122 hits out of 9,433 shots fired.

By the end of January 1899, the Spanish were gone from Cuba. A United States army of occupation ruled the island with a view toward preparing the Cubans for independence. Despite promises that Cuba would be truly free, some of the insurgents were doubtful. "The Americans have embittered the joy of the victors with their forcibly imposed tutelage," the *insurrecto* leader Máximo Gómez said. Still, many insurgent leaders cooperated with the Americans. The Cuban Constitutional Convention of 1900 granted the United States a long-term lease for a naval base at Guantánamo Bay and recognized America's right to intervene in the future to protect the island's independence or to preserve order.

The occupying army could claim one overarching success, a final victory in the long war against yellow fever. In 1900, the U.S. Army Yellow Fever Commission, testing a theory advanced by a Cuban physician, Carlos J. Finley, conclusively demonstrated that a bite of the female *Aëdes aegypti* mosquito transmitted the infection. Gen. Leonard Wood, the one-time Rough Rider colonel who commanded the U.S. occupation forces, oversaw the near-eradication of the disease. There were 1,400 yellow fever cases in Havana alone in 1900. During the following year, after the successful American offensive against mosquito breeding grounds, only 37 cases were reported in all of Cuba. In the United States as well as in Cuba and other tropical nations, the dreaded regular summer and autumn outbreaks of yellow fever gradually became a relic of the past. The last yellow fever epidemic in the United States occurred in New Orleans in 1905.

Rid of the Spanish and free of yellow fever, Cuba in 1902 attained independence, subject to the Platt Amendment. This American law, incorporated into the final U.S.-Cuba treaty of independence, allowed for close U.S. supervision of the island's affairs. Under its provisions, American troops returned briefly in 1906. The Platt Amendment remained in effect until 1934, when the Cuban government successfully demanded its repeal.

In the Philippines, the insurgents and American troops would wage furious war for nearly three years. In March 1899, Congress issued a call for 35,000 volunteers to help suppress the insurrection. A vocal minority of Americans passionately opposed the effort to subdue Aguinaldo's forces. "Every one who believes in the Divine government of the world must believe that God will eventually take up the case of fellows who set unnecessary wars on foot, and I hope he won't forgive them," wrote E. L. Godkin, the editor of the *Nation*. Nor had Andrew Carnegie reconciled himself to annexation. "It's a matter of congratulation that you seem to have about finished your work of civilizing the Filipinos," he wrote to Whitelaw Reid, the editor of the *New York Tribune* and a leading imperialist. "It is thought that about 8,000 of them have been completely civilized and sent to heaven. I hope you like it." By the end of 1899, the United States had 65,000 troops in the Philippines.

Each side accused the other of torture and atrocity. There were claims that the Americans took no prisoners, and the Filipino casualty ratio of five men dead in battle to one wounded seemed to support the charge. U.S. troops condemned the Filipino hit-and-run tactics as vicious and unsporting. "With an enemy like this to fight, it is not surprising that the boys should soon adopt 'no quarter' as a motto, and fill the blacks full of lead before finding out whether they are friends or enemies," ran a soldier's letter quoted in one of the Anti-imperialist League publications.

Much to the insurgents' dismay, the Philippine war did not become an issue in the U.S. presidential campaign of 1900, in which President McKinley won reelection over the Nebraska volunteer colonel William Jennings Bryan. "We have failed to waken the lethargic American conscience," Aguinaldo said. In December, just a month after the election, the U.S. troops surprised Aguinaldo's headquarters in the Luzon mountain village of Palanan and arrested the insurgent leader.

Even so, the war ground on. On September 28, 1901, Filipino forces ambushed a Ninth Infantry detachment at breakfast near Balangiga on the island of Samar. Forty-eight Americans were killed, many of them hacked to pieces with bolo knives. Theodore Roosevelt, who had parlayed his Rough Rider fame into the Republican vice presidential nomination in 1900 and had just recently succeeded to the presidency after McKinley's assassination, ordered "the most stern policies" in reprisal. The U.S. commander in Samar, Gen. Jacob Smith, instructed his troops to convert the island into a "howling wilderness," to "create in the minds of all the people a burning desire for the war to cease." Smith sanctioned the burning of villages and crops, the torture of prisoners, and the execution of insurgents. His excesses led to his eventual court-martial, though his only punishment was a forced early retirement from the army.

In July 1901, an American-run Philippine Civil Commission took over from the U.S. military the work of establishing local government, schools, and public services throughout the archipelago. By July 1902,

General Aguinaldo and 10 of the delegates to the first Assembly of Representatives in 1929 *(Library of Congress, Prints and Photographs Division [LC-USZ62-120614])*

U.S. artillery soldiers ride down a street in Malolos during the Philippine Insurrection, 1899 *(Library of Congress, Prints & Photographs Division [LC-USZ62-114970])*

American pacification methods had become so successful that the War Department could declare the insurgency at an end. The final cost of pacifying the Philippines was perhaps never calculated, but it greatly exceeded the $20 million cession fee paid to Spain. Moreover, some 20,000 Filipino insurgents had been killed in battle. As many as 200,000 civilians were dead of hunger, disease, or other indirect results of the insurrection.

The Spanish-American War and its aftermath wrought enormous changes in America's role in the world. For the first time, the United States achieved the status of a world power, acquiring colonial posses-sions in the Caribbean and the Pacific and accepting a major role in the tangled international politics of China and its neighbors. The war cemented American-British friendship, what would come to be known as the "special relationship," which would be tested and strengthened by

President McKinley and Admiral Dewey review troops, Washington, D.C., October 3, 1899. *(Library of Congress)*

two world wars. It also increased political pressure for an isthmian canal linking the Caribbean and the Pacific. Work on the Panama Canal would begin in 1904.

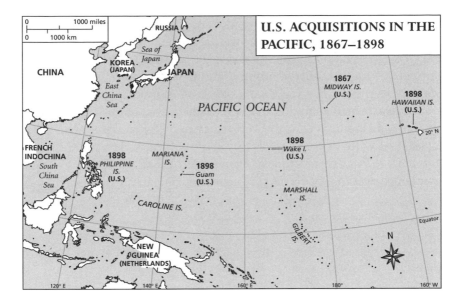

The anti-imperialists were beaten on the Philippine question, but they and their heirs, the isolationists, would continue to raise a strong dissenting voice in American foreign policy for decades to come. Wearied by colonial wars, uninterested in European conflicts, preoccupied by domestic issues, many Americans found themselves repeating the question the anonymous author of this bit of newspaper doggerel addressed to the poet and imperial publicist Rudyard Kipling:

> We've taken up the white man's burden
> of ebony and brown;
> Now will you tell us, Rudyard,
> how we may put it down?

The Americans remained in control of the Philippines until Japanese military forces overran the archipelago in 1942. Two years later, an American offensive regained the islands. In 1946, the year after World War II ended, and with colonialism everywhere in retreat, the Filipinos achieved their independence at last. Emilio Aguinaldo survived to see the realization of his dream, the Philippine Republic. The one-time insurgent leader lived on until 1964, full of years and honor and long since reconciled to the American colonial interlude.

Thus the far-reaching consequences of the sinking of the battleship *Maine* were revealed over the decades. Salvage teams raised the warship's hulk from the Havana harbor mud in 1911, and a new investigation confirmed the original court of inquiry finding that a submerged mine had destroyed it. Sixty-five years later, American naval engineers, working with sophisticated computer models, reached what doubtless will stand as the final explanation for the *Maine* disaster. "The available evidence is consistent with an internal explosion alone," Adm. Hyman Rickover wrote in 1976. "The most likely source was heat from a fire in the coal bunker adjacent to the six-inch reserve magazine."

Glossary

anti-imperialist In American politics, an opponent of U.S. acquisition of overseas territory such as Hawaii (1896) and the Philippines (1900). Anti-imperialists regarded colonies as immoral and unconstitutional; some also opposed them on the grounds they would add to the nonwhite population of the United States.

black powder An obsolescent explosive, it discharged a dark smoke cloud when ignited. With not enough smokeless powder to go around, most volunteer units were supplied with black powder; they complained that the cloud gave away their positions to the Spanish.

blockade Isolating a port, city, region, or nation by surrounding it with ships or troops to prevent the passage of traffic or supplies.

blockhouse A small defensive structure, often built of concrete and fitted out with a garrison. The Spanish forces built blockhouses in Cuba in an effort to protect towns and sugar plantations and to impede the movement of Cuban insurgent columns.

bluejacket A nickname for an enlisted man in the U.S. Navy.

bolo A Spanish word based on a Philippine name for a long, single-edged, broad knife.

brigade A unit of military organization, composed of two or more regiments. Two or more brigades made up a division. U.S. brigades are styled by arabic numeral.

bunker A compartment or tank on a ship used for storing fuel.

corps A large body of troops, usually of three divisions and composed of all the elements—infantry, cavalry, and artillery—that make up an army. The U.S. Army mobilized eight corps in 1898. The U.S. expeditionary force that landed in Cuba bore the designation of V Corps. The I Corps saw action in Puerto Rico, the VIII Corps in the Philippines.

division   A large formation of infantry or cavalry, formed when two or more brigades are linked together under a single command.

flag of truce   A flag, usually white, carried when a peaceful communication or message is to be delivered to an enemy. The Americans and the Spanish at Santiago discussed surrender terms under numerous flags of truce in July 1898.

Gatling gun   Named for its American inventor, Robert J. Gatling (1808–1903), this early machine gun fired multiple small-caliber projectiles from a cluster of rotating barrels. With a maximum rate of fire of 600 rounds a minute, the Gatling remained in use in the U.S. Army and U.S. Navy through the Spanish-American War.

insurrectos   Spanish for "insurgents" or "insurrectionaries," the name by which Cubans fighting for independence from Spain after 1895 were known.

jingo   An aggressive patriot, one who favors a warlike posture in foreign relations. Originally a word used simply to express emphasis ("By jingo!"), its special application derived from an English music hall refrain of 1878. It was used to refer to Americans who called for retribution against Spain after a mysterious explosion destroyed the battleship USS *Maine* in Havana harbor in 1898.

machete   A Spanish word which has entered the English language, the diminutive for *macho* (hammer), it refers to a large knife with a broad blade; it is used for cutting vegetation but may also be used as a weapon.

magazine   Aboard a warship, the sealed-off compartment in which explosives are stored.

malaria   From the Italian for "bad air," a mosquito-borne intermittent infectious disease marked by high fever and chills. Malaria debilitated U.S. troops in Cuba in the summer of 1898. Some veterans of the campaign suffered recurrent attacks for many years after the end of the war.

man-of-war   A warship, usually a large one such as a battleship.

monitor   Generic designation for an armored warship with a flat deck and carrying one or two great guns in a revolving turret. The name was coined by John Ericsson, the inventor of the first of these vessels during the Civil War, the U.S.S. *Monitor*. It is based on the Latin "to admonish." By 1898 monitors were obsolete, although four served in Cuban waters as blockade auxiliaries and for shore bombardment. Two others crossed the Pacific to reinforce the U.S. squadron in the Philippines.

quarantine Any isolation or restriction on travel with the aim of preventing the spread of infectious diseases. Originally the period was 40 days. The word is derived from the Italian word for 40, *quaranta.*

reconcentration After 1895, Spain's policy of concentrating country people in towns and fortified places to deny aid and supplies to Cuban insurgent forces. It was widely regarded as inhumane.

regiment A basic unit of military organization, an infantry regiment contained 10 companies. Volunteer regiments were recruited by state and so designated; (e.g., the Seventy-first New York.) A regiment's authorized strength was about 1,000 men.

siege An army's painstaking sealing off of a town or a fortress from all outside contacts and supplies for the purpose of bringing its residents to surrender without requiring the force of arms. American forces besieged Santiago in July 1898 and ultimately forced its capitulation without a full-scale battle.

skirmish A small battle usually involving small forces but sometimes referring to an engagement where large forces are avoiding more direct conflict.

strategy The science of planning and directing large-scale military movements designed to bring about the defeat of an enemy.

superstructure Those parts of a ship that rise above the main deck.

tactics The arranging, deployment, and maneuvering of troops in battle, usually in pursuit of a short-range objective such as capturing a position.

trocha The Spanish word for a pathway or track, it was applied to part of Spain's defensive system in the war against the Cuban insurgency from 1895–98. A *trocha* usually involved a wide cleared belt, electrically illuminated at night, with garrisoned forts and blockhouses at regular intervals. Spain used the *trocha* system in tandem with its policy of reconcentration of Cuba's rural population. In theory, the strategy would deny freedom of movement, supplies, and shelter to the enemy.

turret A low, revolving armored structure that houses a warship's big guns. The most powerful U.S. battleships carried four 13-inch guns mounted in heavily armored turrets fore and aft.

yellow fever A deadly infectious tropical disease, it is caused by a virus transmitted by the bite of the *Aëdes aegypti* mosquito. High fever, intense muscle and joint pain, jaundice, and vomiting are symptoms of the disease. The yellow flag used to announce a fever quarantine was known as the "yellow jack."

yellow journalism A term applied to newspapers that printed sensational and scandalous stories, what later would be called "tabloid journalism." The term came from the color of ink used to print what is recognized as the first comic strip, "The Yellow Kid." Its originator, Richard Outcault, introduced the strip in the *World* (1895) but then took it to the *Journal* when offered more money. When the *World* hired someone else to feature the same character in a strip, the two papers became known as the "Yellow Kid papers." Because of their competition with sensational stories, the term evolved into "yellow journalism."

Further Reading

NONFICTION

Azoy, A. C. M. *Charge! The Story of the Battle of San Juan Hill.* New York: Longmans, Green, 1961.

Bierce, Ambrose. *Skepticism and Dissent: Selected Journalism, 1899–1901.* Edited by Lawrence I. Berkove. Ann Arbor, Mich.: UMI Research Press, 1986.

Blow, Michael. *A Ship to Remember: The Maine and the Spanish-American War.* New York: William Morrow, 1992.

Bradford, James, ed. *Crucible of Empire: The Spanish-American War and Its Aftermath.* Annapolis, Md.: Naval Institute Press, 1993.

Brands, H. W. *The Reckless Decade: America in the 1890s.* New York: St. Martin's Press, 1995.

Cashin, Herschel V., and others. *Under Fire with the Tenth U.S. Cavalry.* New York: Arno Press, 1969.

Churchill, Winston S. *A Roving Commission: My Early Life.* New York: Scribner's, 1930.

Damiani, Brian. *Advocates of Empire: William McKinley, the Senate, and American Expansion, 1898–1899.* New York: Garland, 1987.

Davis, Richard Harding. *The Cuban and Porto Rico Campaigns.* New York: Scribner's, 1898.

Dewey, George. *Autobiography.* New York: Scribner's, 1913.

Evans, Robley D. *A Sailor's Log: Recollections of Forty Years of Naval Life.* New York: D. Appleton and Company, 1901.

Feuer, A. B. *The Spanish-American War at Sea: Naval Action in the Atlantic.* Westport, Conn.: Praeger, 1995.

Foner, Philip. *The Spanish-Cuban-American War and the Birth of American Imperialism.* New York: Monthly Review Press, 1972.

Friedel, Frank. *The Splendid Little War.* Boston: Little, Brown, 1959.

Jeffers, Paul H. *Colonel Roosevelt: Theodore Roosevelt Goes to War, 1897–1898.* New York: John Wiley and Sons, 1996.

Jones, Virgil Carrington. *Roosevelt's Rough Riders.* New York: Doubleday, 1971.

Leech, Margaret. *In the Days of McKinley.* New York: Harper, 1969.

Linderman, Gerald R. *The Mirror of War: American Society and the Spanish-American War.* Ann Arbor: University of Michigan Press, 1974.

Lynck, Miles V. *The Black Troopers, Or: The Daring Heroism of Negro Soldiers in the Spanish-American War.* New York: AMS Press, 1971.

May, Ernest R. *Imperial Democracy.* New York: Harcourt, Brace, 1961.

Miller, Richard H., ed. *American Imperialism in 1898: The Quest for National Fulfillment.* New York: Wiley, 1970.

Millis, Walter. *The Martial Spirit.* Boston: Houghton-Mifflin, 1931.

Milton, Joyce. *The Yellow Kids: Foreign Correspondents in the Heyday of Yellow Journalism.* New York: Harper & Row, 1989.

Morgan, Wayne H. *America's Road to Empire: The War with Spain and Overseas Expansion.* New York: John Wiley and Sons, 1965.

Morris, Edmund. *The Rise of Theodore Roosevelt.* New York: Modern Library, 2001.

Musicant, Ivan. *Empire by Default: The Spanish-American War and the Dawn of the American Century.* New York: Henry Holt and Company, 1998.

O'Toole, G. J. A. *The Spanish War.* New York: W. W. Norton, 1984.

Painter, Nell I. *Standing at Armageddon: The United States, 1877–1919.* New York: W. W. Norton, 1987.

Pérez, Louis A. *The War of 1898: The United States and Cuba in History and Historiography.* Chapel Hill: University of North Carolina Press, 1998.

Post, Charles. *The Little War of Private Post: The Spanish-American War Seen Up Close.* Norman: University of Oklahoma Press, 1999.

Rickover, Hyman G. *How the Battleship Maine Was Destroyed.* Washington, D.C.: U.S. Government Printing Office, 1976.

Roosevelt, Theodore. *The Rough Riders.* New York: Scribner's, 1898.

Samuels, Peggy, and Harold Samuels. *Teddy Roosevelt at San Juan: The Making of a President.* College Station: Texas A&M University Press, 1997.

Trask, David. *The War with Spain in 1898.* New York: Macmillan, 1981.

Traxel, David. *1898: The Birth of the American Century.* New York: Alfred A. Knopf, 1998.

Walker, Dale. *The Boys of '98: Theodore Roosevelt and the Rough Riders.* New York: Forge Books, 1998.

Williams, William Appleman. *The Tragedy of American Diplomacy.* New York: Dell Publishing Co., 1962.

FICTION

Crane, Stephen. *Prose and Poetry.* New York: The Library of America, 1984. Includes the following short stories based on his experiences covering the wars in Cuba: "The Prince of the Harness," "The Lone Charge of William B. Perkins," "Flanagan and His Short Filibustering Adventure,"

"The Majestic Lie," "Virtue in War," "Marines Signalling Under Fire at Guantanamo," "God Rest Ye, Merry Gentlemen," "The Sergeant's Private Madhouse," "The Revenge of *Adolphus,*" "The Clan of No-Name." "The Second Generation."

Gowan, Al. *Santiago Rag.* Cambridge, Mass.: Access Press, 1998.

Jones, Douglas. *Remember Santiago.* New York: Henry Holt, 1988.

Leonard, Elmore. *Cuba Libre.* New York: Delacorte Press, 1998.

WEBSITES

Events: Spanish-American War. Available online. URL: http://www. history.navy.mil/photos/events/spanam/eve-pge.htm. Downloaded on May 7, 2002.

New York Public Library Online Exhibition of the Spanish-American War. Available online. URL: http://www.nypl.org/research/chss/epo/spanexhib/. Downloaded on May 7, 2002.

The Spanish-American War Centennial Website. Available online. URL: http://www.spanamwar.com/. Downloaded on May 7, 2002.

The World of 1898: The Spanish-American War. Available online. URL: http://www.loc.gov/rr/hispanic/1898/. Downloaded on May 7, 2002.

Index

Page numbers in *italics* indicate a photograph. Page numbers followed by *m* indicate maps. Page numbers followed by *g* indicate glossary entries. Page numbers in **boldface** indicate box features.